Higher Education

Continuing Education and Training and the EU Framework on State Aid

IMPLICATIONS FOR THE PUBLIC HIGHER EDUCATION SECTOR IN BRANDENBURG

This work is published under the responsibility of the Secretary-General of the OECD. The opinions expressed and arguments employed herein do not necessarily reflect the official views of the Member countries of the OECD.

The project "Analysis and advice for a renewed tertiary education strategy for Brandenburg and guidance on categorisation of scientific continuing education" was funded by the European Union via the Structural Reform Support Programme (REFORM/IM2020/004). This publication was produced with the financial assistance of the European Union. The views expressed herein can in no way be taken to reflect the official opinion of the European Union.

This document, as well as any data and map included herein, are without prejudice to the status of or sovereignty over any territory, to the delimitation of international frontiers and boundaries and to the name of any territory, city or area.

Please cite this publication as:
OECD (2022), *Continuing Education and Training and the EU Framework on State Aid: Implications for the Public Higher Education Sector in Brandenburg*, Higher Education, OECD Publishing, Paris, https://doi.org/10.1787/9ec6cb98-en.

ISBN 978-92-64-38461-3 (print)
ISBN 978-92-64-81571-1 (pdf)
ISBN 978-92-64-60687-6 (HTML)
ISBN 978-92-64-89044-2 (epub)

Higher Education
ISSN 2616-9169 (print)
ISSN 2616-9177 (online)

Photo credits: Cover © elettaria/Shutterstock.com; Cover Illustration: Christophe Brilhault.

Corrigenda to publications may be found on line at: www.oecd.org/about/publishing/corrigenda.htm.
© OECD 2022

The use of this work, whether digital or print, is governed by the Terms and Conditions to be found at https://www.oecd.org/termsandconditions.

Foreword

Ageing populations and rising skill demands have heightened expectations that higher education systems will widen their offer of continuing education and training (CET) for adults aiming to renew or augment their skills at an advanced level. CET is becoming increasingly important for maintaining a highly skilled workforce in Germany, and particularly in the state of Brandenburg in support of the undergoing structural change of its economy. Coal production in Brandenburg is being phased out, while the state government is seeking to encourage the development of advanced manufacturing and to increase the capacity for innovation activity. These developments will likely increase the demand in the labour market for high-level skills. At the same time, Brandenburg's workforce is ageing; its people will likely be expected to participate longer in the labour market than in past.

However, Brandenburg's public higher education institutions have so far been only marginal providers. To expand their offer of CET, they require more legal certainty about the use of public funding in light of European Union (EU) state aid policy. EU state aid policy ensures public subsidies (state aid) are not used by state agencies to crowd out markets (economic activity). There are no clear EU, federal or state-level directions about whether CET is a non-economic activity and thus exempt from EU state aid rules.

This report analyses the reasons for this legal uncertainty and provides recommendations to the state government and public higher education institutions in Brandenburg about how to clarify the status of CET as a state-aided activity. It also proposes pointers for interpretation and future reform of the EU framework on state aid with respect to CET, and provides impulses for policy action in other German states and at the federal level.

The OECD project team commissioned a legal analysis of this question to KPMG Law. KPMG Law was asked to investigate how the different categories of education and training are reflected in the EU legal framework and to develop recommendations aimed at increasing legal certainty. The OECD project team further engaged a German tax expert on higher education institution operations to advise the work. This report benefited substantially from feedback and comments received from Bernhard von Wendland, a senior expert on state aid law and research and innovation policy from the European Commission.

This report is an output of the project "Analysis and advice for a renewed tertiary education strategy for Brandenburg and guidance on categorisation of scientific continuing education", which consisted of two sub-projects and was funded by the EU through the Structural Reform Support Programme. The application for funding of the sub-project on categorisation of CET in higher education was submitted by the University of Applied Sciences Potsdam (*Fachhochschule Potsdam, FH Potsdam*) on the initiative of its President, Prof. Dr. Eva Schmitt-Rodermund, in agreement with the other seven public HEIs in Brandenburg and the Ministry for Science, Research and Culture of the State of Brandenburg (*Ministerium für Wissenschaft, Forschung und Kultur, MWFK*). The project was conducted in close collaboration with FH Potsdam, the state's seven other public HEIs, MWFK, and the Directorate General for Structural Reform Support of the European Commission.

Acknowledgements

This publication is part of the OECD programme of work on higher education policy and was produced with the financial assistance of the European Union.

The OECD project team is grateful for the support of Thomas Pritzkow at the European Commission's Directorate-General for Structural Reform Support (DG REFORM), Rainald Wurzer at the University of Applied Sciences Potsdam (*FH Potsdam*), and Joscha Dapper and Dr. Marko Müller at the Ministry for Science, Research, and Culture of the State of Brandenburg (*Ministerium für Wissenschaft, Forschung, und Kultur, MWFK*). Together with the OECD project team, the DG REFORM, FH Potsdam and MWFK teams formed the advisory group for the project "Analysis and advice for a renewed tertiary education strategy for Brandenburg and guidance on categorisation of scientific continuing education", setting the direction for the project and providing regular advice and feedback on the project's activities and outputs.

The OECD project team is particularly grateful to Dr. Moritz Püstow, Dr. Jannike Ehlers, and Björn Zunker, respectively Partner, Senior Associate and Associate, at KPMG Law Rechtsanwaltsgesellschaft mbH for providing an excellent initial draft of this report and taking the time to participate and share their legal expertise in numerous meetings involving HEIs, EC and MWFK organised within the framework of the project. The OECD project team commissioned KPMG Law to investigate how the different categories of continuing education and training are reflected in the EU legal framework and to develop recommendations aimed at increasing legal certainty.

Special thanks also go to Horst Rambau, a German tax advisor with expertise on HEI operations from Rambau & Ilgart Partnerschaft mbB, and Bernhard von Wendland from the European Commission, a senior expert on state aid law and research and innovation policy, for advising the OECD project team and KPMG Law in the preparation of this report. Horst Rambau developed a first draft of the questionnaire to HEIs, drafted a note on the legal and tax framework governing the provision of CET in Brandenburg, and participated in several meetings organised along the project. Bernhard von Wendland kindly shared his authoritative knowledge of state aid policy as related to higher education in two meetings and through in-depth feedback and comments on the initial draft of this report.

The OECD project team is also thankful to the Presidents and Vice-presidents of Brandenburg's eight public HEIs – Brandenburg University of Technology Cottbus-Senftenberg, European University Viadrina Frankfurt/Oder, Film University Babelsberg Konrad Wolf, University of Potsdam, Brandenburg University of Applied Sciences, University for Sustainable Development Eberswalde, University of Applied Sciences Potsdam, and Technical University of Applied Sciences Wildau – and their staff responsible for continuing education and training for sharing their time and insights during the project's workshop or in individual interviews.

The OECD project team would further like to thank the Federal Ministry of Education and Research (*Bundesministerium für Bildung und Forschung*) and the German Rector's Conference (*Hochschulrektorenkonferenz*) for sharing their important insights about continuing education and training at German HEIs in individual interviews. The OECD project team would like to also thank experts from the

European Commission's Directorate-General for Competition for commenting on the initial draft of this report.

This report was prepared by the OECD's Directorate for Education and Skills using extensively the initial draft developed by KPMG Law. Margarita Kalamova was the project leader responsible for co-ordinating the study, jointly with Rainald Wurzer from FH Potsdam. Thomas Weko, Senior Analyst and Team Leader, Higher Education Policy team, Paulo Santiago, Head of the Policy Advice and Implementation Division in the Directorate of Education and Skills, and Andreas Schleicher, Director for Education and Skills, reviewed the publication.

Timothy Jones translated the initial version of the report from German into English. Roger Smyth and Cassandra Morley edited the report; Cécile Bily and Marika Prince provided administrative support to the project. Cassandra Morley and Rachel Linden assisted with the publication processes.

Table of contents

Foreword	3
Acknowledgements	5
Executive summary	9
1 Introduction	**11**
The context in Brandenburg	12
The aims of this study	12
CET in Germany	13
The hierarchy of law relating to CET	16
Legal basis of European education policy	17
References	21
Notes	22
2 Legal analysis of the regulation of state aid in the EU	**23**
The purpose and defining conditions of the prohibition on state aid	24
Defining conditions of the prohibition on state aid	24
The levels of EU rules on state aid	26
Exclusions and exceptions	27
Consequences of incompatibility of aid	28
The prohibition of cross subsidies and requirement for separate accounting under EU state aid rules	28
References	30
Notes	31
3 Classifying continuing education and training under EU state aid law	**33**
Classification of CET as economic or non-economic	34
The role of the EC in classification	39
Interpretation of EU state aid rules in the KMK Guidelines	44
Assessment of CET against the classification criteria	48
Further defining criteria in prohibition of state aid	50
Interim conclusion on classifying CET in terms of EU state aid rules	60
References	62
Notes	64
4 CET in practice at HEIs in Brandenburg	**67**
The situation at Brandenburg's HEIs	68

Classification of CET offered in other *Länder*	73
References	76
Notes	76

5 Recommendations 77

Introduction	78
Proposal to the EC	79
Standardisation of the individual case assessment at HEIs	80
Developing a guideline for the *Land* Brandenburg	84
Pre-notification, notification and registration of the guideline to the EC	87
References	89
Notes	90

Annex A. Cost accounting approaches 91

Background	91
Permissibility of the "backwards from the end" approach	91
Assessment in accordance with the principles of separate accounting	92
References	94
Notes	94

Tables

Table 1.1. Categorisation of German CET	14

Figures

Figure 2.1. Levels of state aid under EU law – the example of HEI activities	26
Figure 5.1. Assessment chart for HEIs on the criteria to be reviewed when classifying a CET offering	81

Boxes

Box 3.1. ECJ cases on education, considered as a service	35
Box 3.2. Decisions of the EC on the economic or non-economic classification of education	40
Box 3.3. Cases on the application of state aid rules to higher education decided by the EC	43
Box 3.4. Exemption from the prohibition on state aid under the GBER	55
Box 3.5. Classification of CET as a Service of General Economic Interest (SGEI)	58
Box 5.1. Procedure of the notification of the guideline to the EC	87

Follow OECD Publications on:

http://twitter.com/OECD_Pubs
http://www.facebook.com/OECDPublications
http://www.linkedin.com/groups/OECD-Publications-4645871
http://www.youtube.com/oecdilibrary
http://www.oecd.org/oecddirect/

Executive summary

Brandenburg's economy is undergoing structural change. Coal production in the state is being phased out, while the state government is seeking to encourage the development of advanced manufacturing and to increase the capacity for innovative activity. At the same time, Brandenburg's workforce is ageing; its people will likely be expected to participate longer in the labour market than in past. Overall, the structural change will likely bring considerable technological and societal changes and these developments will likely increase the demand in the labour market for high-level skills.

Continuing education and training (CET) is thus becoming increasingly important for maintaining a highly skilled workforce in the state of Brandenburg. This heightens expectations that Brandenburg's higher education system will widen its CET offer for adults aiming to renew or augment their skills at an advanced level. However, Brandenburg's public higher education institutions (HEIs) have so far been only marginal providers. One of the constraints on the development of a greater focus on CET is the uncertainty about the use of their public resources for CET programmes in light of European Union (EU) state aid policy.

This report analyses the reasons for this legal uncertainty and provides recommendations to the state government and public HEIs in Brandenburg about how to deal with the issue of state aid law. It also provides suggestions for a potential future reform of the EU framework on state aid.

The problem

HEIs considering using their public resources for CET need to do so in the light of EU state aid rules. EU state aid policy should ensure public subsidies (state aid) are not used by firms to compete unfairly, or by state agencies to crowd out markets (economic activity). CET is defined in the Brandenburg Higher Education Act as a statutory duty of state HEIs, as with undergraduate education and research. HEI research and undergraduate education are classified as non-economic activities and are not subject to EU state aid rules. However, neither the European Commission (EC) nor the European Court of Justice (ECJ) has provided any clear directions about whether CET can be considered a non-economic activity and thus exempt from EU state aid rules. Presently, individual CET programmes are judged on a case-by-case basis as economic or non-economic. The relevant federal body, the Assembly of Ministers of Education of German states (*Kultusministerkonferenz*), has not provided sufficient clarity on state aid questions either.

HEIs risk being out of conformity with EU state aid rules, which may result in base funding being reclaimed. As a result, HEIs in Brandenburg tend to avoid offering CET, or do so only in the high-price segment or by managing the risks through associated institutes.

This report contains a legal analysis (commissioned by the OECD project team to KPMG Law) of the EU law on state aid as related to CET in higher education.

The analysis begins with an examination of whether, and under what circumstances, a CET programme should be regarded as an economic activity. It then considers cases where a programme is an economic activity but contains features that may lead to exemptions and exceptions from state aid rules. As part of the analysis, seven of Brandenburg's eight public HEIs provided information on their current CET offerings.

These offerings are assessed using the criteria and principles that came out of the analysis. Finally, the report develops a decision-making framework that would make it easier for HEIs to conduct a systematic analysis of a CET programme against the rules on EU state aid, taking account of ECJ case law and EC decisions.

Summary of recommendations

This report sets out recommendations – on the basis of the legal analysis – which aim to:

1. Simplify the rules developed by the European Commission for state aid as related to CET in higher education

- The EC should be invited to simplify and clarify state aid rules as they apply to public funding of CET at HEIs.
- The Brandenburg state government should work with the other states (*Länder*) and the federal government to encourage the EC to codify the assessment of CET as an economic or a non-economic activity, following the model used for contract research undertaken by HEIs and codified in the draft Research and Development (R&D) Framework.

2. Standardise the individual case assessment at higher education institutions

- HEIs should adopt a standardised process for the classification of CET programmes drawn from the case law of the ECJ and the administrative practice of the EC and should set prices/fees for CET programmes in conformity with EU state aid rules.
- HEIs should document in detail their decision-making processes on the classification of CET programmes and on the costing and fee setting for programmes.

3. Develop a guideline for the Land Brandenburg

- The Ministry for Science, Research and Culture of the State of Brandenburg (*Ministerium für Wissenschaft, Forschung und Kultur, MWFK*) should formulate a guideline that would outline the classification process for CET programmes, the structure of a CET offering that complies with EU state aid rules and the possible exceptions to and exemptions from the prohibition of state aid that may be applicable.
- MWFK should submit this guideline to the EC for notification.

1 Introduction

Continuing education and training (CET) is of growing importance to the German economy and, in particular, to the economy of Brandenburg; the ageing population and the advances of automation and other forms of technology mean that workers will need to update their skills frequently in the future, as skills demand evolves and changes. However, the complexities of European law – and especially, the EU state aid rules – mean that the state government and Brandenburg's higher education institutions (HEIs) are uncertain about the legality of public funding of CET. This poses risks of under-investment in CET – which, in turn, poses risks for workforce development. The OECD project team has commissioned an analysis of the legal constraints of funding for CET, which is set out in this report.

The context in Brandenburg

The German federal state of Brandenburg is one of the former East German states (the new *Länder*). The state surrounds the federal capital, Berlin, and the state capital, Potsdam, borders Berlin.

The state's economy is undergoing structural change that will open new opportunities for highly skilled people. Coal production in the state is being phased out, while the state government is seeking to encourage the development of advanced manufacturing and to increase the capacity for innovative activity. These developments will likely increase the demand in the labour market for high-level skills.

At the same time, Brandenburg's population of 2.5 million is one of the oldest among the German states and the average age is forecast to increase further (Statistik Berlin-Brandenburg, 2021[1]). One consequence of this demographic change is that people are likely to remain longer in the workforce compared to in past, and will face a higher probability of changes in the nature of their work.

Alongside these changes, the workforce of Brandenburg – like the rest of Germany and all advanced economies – faces significant changes in their work roles as new technologies, automation and artificial intelligence change the nature of work. This digital transformation of work means that job requirements and the skills required for work will change (BMAS, 2020[2]). The OECD estimates that Germany is one of the countries most affected by this sort of change, with around 50% of all jobs subject to a significant degree of automation (Nedelkoska and Quintini, 2018[3]).

These changes mean that, throughout the workforce, the skills required for the majority of jobs – and, by implication, the need for continuing education and training (CET) – will change and increase (OECD, 2021[4]).

However, Brandenburg's public higher education institutions (HEIs) have so far been only marginal providers of CET. In order to expand their offer of CET, they would require more legal certainty about the use of their publicly funded resources in light of European Union (EU) state aid policy. This study does not call for more public funding for CET. Although additional public funding is desirable (Wissenschaftsrat, 2019[5]), it is not the focus of this study and is therefore not part of the recommendations.

The aims of this study

The aims of this study are to classify CET programmes offered by Brandenburg's HEIs in the light of the EU's legal framework on state aid and to identify opportunities to use publicly funded resources for CET programmes.

The OECD project team commissioned a legal analysis of this question by KPMG Law. KPMG Law was asked to investigate how the different categories of education and training are reflected in the EU legal framework and to develop recommendations aimed at increasing legal certainty. The OECD project team further engaged a tax expert on HEI operations and collaborated with a senior expert on state aid law and research and innovation policy from the European Commission (EC). They both provided valuable advice for this work.

The study was part of the project "Analysis and advice for a renewed tertiary education strategy for Brandenburg and guidance on categorisation of scientific continuing education", funded by the EC through the Structural Reform Support Programme. The application for funding of the sub-project on categorisation of continuing education and training was submitted by the University of Applied Sciences Potsdam (*Fachhochschule Potsdam, FH Potsdam*) on the initiative of ist President, Prof. Dr. Eva Schmitt-Rodermund, in agreement with the other seven public HEIs in Brandenburg and the Ministry for Science, Research and Culture of the State of Brandenburg (*Ministerium für Wissenschaft, Forschung und Kultur, MWFK*). The project was conducted in close collaboration with FH Potsdam, the other seven public state's

HEIs, MWFK, and the Directorate-General for Structural Reform Support of the EC. This report presents the results of that investigation:

- Chapter 1 describes the growing importance of CET in helping firms deal with the changing skills needs in Germany, and particularly in Brandenburg, and sketches the framework around the provision of CET.
- Chapter 2 lays out the European legal framework for regulating state aid.
- Chapter 3 analyses the requirements a CET programme must meet to be considered for a government subsidy under EU law, notes that the status of CET under that legal framework is not clear and explores the case law to identify principles that give guidance on the interpretation of EU law.
- Chapter 4 describes the application of this legal framework in practice at HEIs in Brandenburg.
- Chapter 5 provides recommendations to the state government and public HEIs in Brandenburg about how to clarify the status of continuing education and training as a state-aided activity. It also proposes pointers for interpretation and future reform of the EU framework on state aid, and provides suggestions for policy action.

CET in Germany

The national skills strategy

The context in Germany and Brandenburg, in particular, means that a necessary condition for economic success is ensuring that workers have the opportunity and the incentive to refresh their skills progressively and continuously over their careers (OECD, 2021[6]). In light of this, the German federal government has established a National Skills Strategy (*Nationale Weiterbildungsstrategie*, NWS). The NWS focuses on CET as a means of lifting vocational capabilities.

The federal government aims to make continuing education and training a natural component of people's careers. The NWS includes a number of objectives relating to CET, for instance:

- increase the transparency and range of CET courses and programmes on offer;
- strengthen the responsibility of social partners in relation to CET;
- strengthen CET advice services for individuals and companies, and increase motivation to engage in CET;
- raise recognition and acceptance of skills acquired by employees through CET;
- develop CET qualifications and a range of programmes on offer;
- assure the qualifications of personnel involved in CET;
- improve CET statistics and strategic planning regarding future skills needs.

In setting the NWS, the federal government has recognised that maintaining, developing and enriching the skills of the workforce is an important national challenge to Germany's future prosperity, and that CET is a key component of addressing that challenge.

The OECD has also acknowledged the role NWS has played in fostering CET:

> "Germany has recently done a lot to modernise its CET landscape and improve the co-ordination of its many CET actors – not least through its National Skills Strategy. This path must be continued and expanded, especially through a stronger focus on those groups whose professional future depends most on continuing education and training" (OECD, 2021[7]).

Benefits of CET

Responsibility for CET is shared by companies, social and economic partners, CET providers and the government at national and federal state level (OECD, 2021[6]). In commenting on the OECD's 2021 study of CET in Germany, Federal Minister of Education and Research, Anja Karliczek, stated:

> "Continuing vocational education and training [berufliche Weiterbildung] is key to maintaining our competitiveness and the innovativeness of our country. Continuing vocational training is an absolute necessity for companies and for employees. It is part of lifelong learning. We have taken important steps towards a new CET culture with the National Skills Strategy… One of the steps we have taken is the improvement of access to CET by expanding basic vocational education and training… we reaffirm the joint responsibility of the business community, the social partners and the federal and state governments for shaping and financing continuing vocational education and training. Setting the right framework conditions remains the central task of policymakers…" (BMBF, 2021[8])

Workers experience benefits from participating in high quality CET – such as greater job satisfaction, lower risk of unemployment, enhanced opportunities for promotion and higher earnings. Likewise, employers benefit from their employees undertaking CET – because, in acquiring greater skill, workers lift their productivity, helping the enterprise to thrive. The comments of the Federal Minister of Education and Research recognise that there is, in addition, a public benefit from lifting the skills of the German workforce through CET. Given that the benefits of CET are shared between employers, employees and the public, there is a case for sharing the costs between those three parties; otherwise, there is a risk of under-investment in CET.

Types of CET and their providers

The take-up of continuing education or training by adults in Germany is slightly above the OECD average (OECD, 2021[4]) – around tenth of OECD countries, with around half of respondents to the Survey of Adult Skills having undertaken some non-formal or formal training in the twelve months before the survey. However, there is a wide range of types and providers of CET (OECD, 2021[6]) (Table 1.1).

Table 1.1. Categorisation of German CET

Type of CET	Categories	Providers
Basic CET	Literacy courses Basic skills courses	Adult Education Centres Education institutes of trade unions Education institutes of churches Private non-profit providers
General CET	Second chance education	Evening schools Adult Education Centres Vocational schools/upper secondary schools Private non-profit providers
Vocational CET	**Initial vocational education and training** **Vocational retraining** **Adjustment measures** **Vocational upskilling**	Vocational schools Inter-company vocational training facilities Private non-profit providers Private commercial providers Enterprises Education institutes of the Chambers Technical Schools
Higher education CET	Bachelor's degrees Master's degrees Non-formal CET in higher education	Universities of Co-operative Education Universities for Public Administration Universities of Applied Sciences Universities Research institutes

Adult liberal education	Culture education	Adult Education Centres (Volkshochschulen)
	Democracy education	Church groups
	Literacy courses	Political foundations
	Basic skills courses	Trade unions
	Vocational CET courses	Commercial private providers
		Non-profit private providers

Source: OECD (2021[6]), *Continuing Education and Training in Germany*, Getting Skills Right, https://doi.org/10.1787/1f552468-en.

There are many types of providers of CET in Germany – around 40% of them are private, some of which are not for profit. Types of providers vary from adult education centres to the education arms of organisations like the chambers. Around 10% of providers are HEIs and vocational education institutions (OECD, 2021[6]).

In order to further strengthen the take-up and offer of CET, (OECD, 2021[6]) has recommended to German policy makers to improve the governance structures in CET; undertake a systematic approach to guidance, validation and partial qualifications; expand funding and bundle financial incentives; and attract adults with low basic skills to CET.

CET in higher education

CET is one of the four core responsibilities of HEIs in Germany, as specified in the 1998 Federal Higher Education Framework Act[1]. Nationally, around 5% of adults aged 18-65 take part in CET in higher education in any given year, according to data from the German adult education survey (OECD, 2021[6]).

However, CET is not uniformly defined on either the federal or the state level. CET is referenced as a function of HEIs in the state higher education laws in various ways, particularly with regard to the purpose and form of the CET programmes:

- The Saxon Higher Education Act (*Sächsisches Hochschulgesetzes*, SächsHG) centres on the purpose of CET: "HEIs offer CET programmes. These are designed to expand specialised knowledge or develop scientific or artistic skills and abilities."
- The State Higher Education Act of Mecklenburg-Western Pomerania (*Landeshochschulgesetz Mecklenburg-Vorpommern*, LHG M-V) describes both the purpose and the concrete range of CET programmes to be offered: "HEIs develop and expand their scientific and artistic continuing education programmes in a manner that is oriented towards target groups and takes into account the requirements of lifelong learning. The CET programmes on offer include master's degree programmes that provide CET; foundational bachelor's degree programmes that provide CET; CET with a certificate of completion; and other CET events and courses. As a rule, the CET courses [at HEIs] are aimed at people with qualified practical professional experience."
- The Hessian Higher Education Act (*Hessisches Hochschulgesetzes*, HessHG) highlights the purpose of the CET programmes: "HEIs are to develop and offer CET programmes to deepen academic knowledge and supplement practical professional experience."

The Standing Conference of the Ministers of Education and Cultural Affairs of the Länder in the Federal Republic of Germany (*Ständige Konferenz der Kultusminister der Länder in der Bundesrepublik Deutschland or Kultusministerkonferenz, KMK*) defines CET as: "the continuation or resumption of organised learning after the completion of a first phase of education and as a rule after the commencement of gainful employment or founding a family, whereby the CET programme selected is on the level of specialisation and didactic approach found at a HEI" (KMK, 2001[9]).

This is a very broad definition. The term "organised learning" can cover a wide range of activities, from a three-week language course to a full master's course. What is important about this definition is that CET in higher education is seen as directed at those who have undertaken (or completed) a first course of education. The definition offered by the KMK is not a statutory definition. However, the KMK is an organisation in which ministers of culture of the *Länder* co-operate as members of government and as such, the content of their reports can be drawn upon at least for the interpretation of terms in acts of law.

In Brandenburg, CET is discussed in the Brandenburg Higher Education Act (*Hochschulgesetz Brandenburg (BbgHG)*). § 25(1) BbgHG also initially defines CET programmes at HEIs in terms of their purpose – they are to serve further scientific, artistic and vocational qualifications, and to train the next generation of academics, scientists, researchers and artists. This content is to be co-ordinated with the rest of the higher education curriculum and is to incorporate practical, professional experience and requirements.

Although the wording of this definition is not the same, the content is the same as in the KMK version. Overall, § 25(1) BbgHG expresses the intention to provide further qualifications (*weitere Qualifikationen*), in other words, the resumption (*Wiederaufnahme*) of education and training. This, in turn, assumes that a first phase has already been concluded. Given that the CET programmes are to be co-ordinated with the rest of the curricula at the HEIs, it follows that the level of specialisation and didactic methods of higher education programmes are to be reflected in the CET offerings. This finding is made particularly clear by the first sentence of § 25(2) BbgHG, which provides that CET leads to a higher education degree (*Hochschulabschluss*) in accordance with the second sentence of § 28(1) BbgHG.

The hierarchy of law relating to CET

Higher education institutions in Germany (*Hochschulen*) are governed according to a network of European, federal and state regulations which protect them while subjecting them to obligations.

Higher education – between Basic Law, state constitutions and European law

The freedom of the sciences in Art. 5(3) of the Basic Law (*Grundgesetz, GG*) protects the activities of research and teaching from undue interference by the state and also provides the foundations upon which institutions of higher education, training and research can be established (Gärditz, 2019[10])[2]. In the understanding of higher education laws of the states (*Länder*), HEIs are a cornerstone supporting the democratic state[3]. For this reason, these institutions are eligible for public funding by the *Länder*.

Art. 31(1) and Art. 32 (1) of the Constitution of the State of Brandenburg (*BbgVerf*) mirror the freedom of the sciences in the Basic Law. Art. 31(1) *BbgVerf* guarantees the freedom of the sciences identically with Art. 5(3) GG, while Art. 32(1) *BbgVerf* includes the right to self-administration for HEIs. HEIs can invoke Art. 31(a) and Art. 32(2) *BbgVerf* and Art. 5(3) GG (Basic Law) to defend themselves against undue interference by other public authorities in their scientific activities and self-administration (Gärditz, 2019[10])[4]. The HEIs are, however, also public authorities and parties obligated to the constitution in all respects save for a state-imposed restriction on the freedom of the sciences. As a result, the HEIs are bound in their actions to the law in accordance with Art. 20(3) GG[5] (Geis, 2020[11]). All European, federal and state laws apply in their valid form in Germany to the HEIs.

European law takes precedence over national law. Therefore, if there is a regulation in European law applicable in a field and if the field has an EU relevance, then the European regulation takes precedence over both statutory regulations and the regulations of the Federal and the state constitutions[6]. The scope for both federal and state legislators to draft new laws is limited in the areas governed by European law (Callies/Kahl/Puttler, 2016[12])[7] and this applies also to the domain of higher education, where European regulations must be given precedence.

Higher education laws are state laws

Since the 2006 reform of the federal system in Germany, higher education laws have been almost exclusively within the legislative competence of the *Länder*[8]. The Higher Education Framework Act (*Hochschulrechtsrahmengesetz*, HRG)[9], last amended in 2007, has not been repealed but is applied only in those fields in which a *Land* has not enacted a new law (Geis, 2020[11])[10]. The *Länder* have amended their own higher education acts since 2006, with the result that the remaining scope of application of the (federal) HRG is narrow (Geis, 2020[11])[11].

The KMK was established in order to co-ordinate higher education legislation in the Federal Republic of Germany. The resolutions of the KMK are not binding on the *Länder*. Rather; the KMK may make recommendations which then require translation into the laws of each of the *Länder* (VGH Baden-Württemberg, 2016[13])[12]. The acts passed by the *Bundestag* and the parliaments of the *Länder* (*Landtage*) hold sway, supplemented by statutory ordinances and by-laws added by subordinate bodies entitled to issue subordinate regulations. These include the HEIs themselves within their right to draw up their own statutes, see e.g. § 5(1) *Hochschulgesetz Brandenburg* (BbgHG).

Higher education budgetary law

General budgetary regulations are set out in the Budgetary Principles Act (*Haushaltsgrundsätzegesetz*, HGrG) and the Federal Budgetary Regulations (*Bundeshaushaltsordnung*). These federal laws are supplemented by regulations in the higher education laws of the *Länder* and higher education statute laws (*Hochschulsatzungsrecht*) (Geis, 2020[11])[13].

The budgetary laws set out the rights of HEIs to be granted funding. While HEIs are primarily funded from the public purse, they may also receive funding from third parties[14]. Third-party sources are typically fees paid by companies to commission research or expert reports, but they may also include fees paid for CET programmes.

How money from third-party sources is used can cause conflict between the HEI's own interests on the one hand and its public function and/or its educational mandate on the other.

The HEIs are also bound by justice and the law (*Recht und Gesetz*) in the same manner as with their third-party funded activities, even though these are generally governed by private law. The applicable prescriptions of EU state aid rules in particular are designed to prevent activities in this area that could lead to a distortion of the market.

Legal basis of European education policy

Because the European Union was established originally as a mechanism to facilitate trade, its primary focus initially was economic. For this reason, for many years, its education focus was vocational education and training (VET) policy. Issues of general education, on the other hand, were less significant until the mid-1980s when the EU introduced exchange programmes for HEIs (the Erasmus scheme). The Treaties of Maastricht and Amsterdam then also gave the EU powers to engage in education and training but stopped short of attempts to harmonise national education systems (Wehling, 2020[14]).

On 1 December 2009, the Treaty of Lisbon came into effect. The Treaty has two parts: the Treaty on European Union (TEU) and the Treaty on the Functioning of the European Union (TFEU). The TFEU sets out rules on the legislative competence of the Union. According to the principle of conferral, in Art. 5(2) TFEU, the EU has only those competences that have been conferred on it by the Member States in the Treaties.

The competences are divided into three main categories:

- exclusive competences;
- shared competences;
- supporting competences.

In areas where the EU has exclusive competence (such as trade) European law has primacy over national law. Where the EU has only *supporting competence,* the EU can implement measures to support, co-ordinate or supplement the measures of the Member States, but the Member States' national law has primacy. In education and training policy, the EU has only supporting competence.

In particular, Arts. 165 and 166 TFEU determine the EU's priorities on education issues. The focus is on promotion programmes and on co-ordinating activities. Art. 165(1) TFEU contains a block on powers, meaning that the responsibility for shaping education policy remains with the Member States.

Instruments in European education policy

The EU has a number of different mechanisms at its disposal to actively shape and steer European education policy, including policy discourse, European benchmarking, monitoring and comparative research. Furthermore, the EU can provide a common direction, for example through recommendations, opinions or conclusions. These include:

- Open Method of Co-ordination (OMC) – a methodology for setting education policy objectives between Member States, offering the possibility of a common political approach.
- Research – where the EU steers policy through its funding of research; its "Horizon Europe 2021-2027" programme includes funding (of EUR 95.5 billion over seven years) and a set of priorities for science and innovation. Its strategy paper, which defines the thematic funding priorities and objectives, does not explicitly mention CET. However, it can be assumed that CET programmes could be used as an instrument for upskilling and reskilling. Particularly due to the many references to already existing structures, the search for progress and the further development of projects already underway, as well as the use of existing institutions and programmes, it can be assumed that CET programmes may also be eligible for funding.
- Policy co-operation (ET-2020) – a set of working groups on general education and vocational training to support common policy objectives. The ET-2020 working group on vocational education and training (VET) and continuing vocational education and training (CVET) focused on digitalisation.[15]

Strategies and developments

The concept of lifelong learning is a recurring theme of European educational policy. The first step towards an adult education strategy came in the form of the EU Commission's Memorandum on Lifelong Learning in 2000, which was presented in the wake of the Lisbon European Council in March 2000. The summit of European heads of state and government adopted a programme that is also referred to as the Lisbon Strategy.

- Lisbon Strategy – Until 2010, the Union had the strategic goal "to become the most competitive and dynamic knowledge-based economy in the world, capable of sustainable economic growth with more and better jobs and greater social cohesion".
- Europe 2020 – The new framework strategy proposed by the EU Commission in March 2010, in the aftermath of the financial crisis, aimed to help the Union emerge stronger from the crisis and transform it into a smart, sustainable and inclusive economy by 2020. Europe 2020 had the goals of i) 75% of the working-age population should be in work, ii) 3% of the EU's Gross Domestic Product (GDP) should be expended on research and development, iii) climate protection/energy targets should be achieved, iv) the proportion of early school leavers should be brought down to

below 10%, and at least 40% of the younger generation should have a higher education degree, and v) the number of people at risk of poverty should fall by 20 million.
- 2020 Council Recommendation on Vocational Education and Training recommended the adoption of vocational education and training for sustainable competitiveness, social fairness and resilience with the following targets to be attained at EU level by 2025: i) at least 82% of VET graduates should be in employment, ii) 60% of young VET graduates should be given the opportunity for work-based learning during their VET and CET programmes, iii) 8% of VET learners should benefit from learning mobility abroad.
- Osnabrück Declaration 2020 takes into account the above-mentioned Council Recommendation and focuses on the following four main areas for the period 2021–2025: i) resilience and excellence through quality, inclusive and flexible VET, ii) establishing a new lifelong learning culture – relevance of CET and digitalisation, iii) sustainability – a green link in VET, and iv) developing a European Education and Training Area and international VET.

EU funding programmes

The EU supports education initiatives in Member States via several EU funding programmes. However, it must always observe the subsidiarity principle in accordance with Article 5(3) TEU, which means that the EU funding measures may not replace the funding measures of the Member States, and so the EU does not as a rule provide 100% of the funding for a project.

The European Social Fund (ESF) and Erasmus+ emerge as the main EU programmes in support of education initiatives:

- European Social Fund (ESF) promotes CET, qualification and work-related training, and also dedicates at least 20% of its resources to promoting social inclusion and reducing poverty and discrimination. Each Member State develops its own funding programmes, taking into account national and regional specificities. The funds are administered decentrally through federal and state ministries, which select the projects for ESF funding. In transition regions, where GDP is between 75% and 90% of the EU average, up to 80% of the cost of a selected project can be supported by ESF funding. The programmes are diverse and are thus intended to be responsive to the different circumstances of those receiving support. In addition to institutionalised programmes organised by federal or state ministries and implemented by private institutions, there is also the possibility of individual funding, where individuals can be supported with funding for a CET programme of their own choice. However, ESF funds are subject to state aid law in the same way as other decentralised EU funds, in particular because Member States have discretionary powers in the selection of beneficiaries.
- Erasmus+ has been in place since 2014 and aims to promote lifelong learning, enable sustainable growth, strengthen social cohesion and European identity, and drive innovation. With a budget of EUR 26.2 billion for the 2021-2027 funding period, the EC focuses on i) inclusion and diversity, ii) digitalisation, iii) environmental protection and sustainability, and iv) internationalisation.

EU rules on state aid

While the EU has only supportive jurisdiction in relation to education policy, the original focus of the Union was to create a common market with fair trade. Anything that distorts competition – for instance, by favouring one player or one group of players in the internal market – contravenes the principle of fair competition and could run counter to the competition rules in the third part of the Treaty on the functioning of the European Union, which aim to prevent distortion of competition.

One effect of this is that if a Member State makes a policy in relation to education (in which the EU has limited jurisdiction) that is deemed to distort a market, then that would represent a breach of the competition rules. For instance, in the case of CET, if a government were to provide funding for some CET providers and exclude others from that funding then that would need to be justified in relation to the competition and state aid rules. If that was found to breach the rules on competition, then the EU would have the right to exact penalties on the Member State.

The broad private offer of CET in Germany makes competition between public and private providers likely to happen in many areas. This has important implications for the classification of CET programmes as economic or non-economic activities under EU state aid rules, as well as the opportunities of using public funding for CET.

References

BMAS (2020), *Nationale Weiterbildungsstrategie*, https://www.bmas.de/DE/Arbeit/Aus-und-Weiterbildung/Weiterbildung/Nationale-Weiterbildungsstrategie/nationale-weiterbildungsstrategie.html. [2]

BMBF (2021), *Press release No 06/2021 from 23.04.2021*, https://www.bmbf.de/bmbf/shareddocs/pressemitteilungen/de/karliczek-weiterbildung-als-sc-novationskraft-weiter-staerken.html. [8]

Calliess/Ruffert (ed.) (2016), *TEU/TFEU, 5. Auflage 2016*. [12]

Geis, M. (ed.) (2020), *Hochschulrecht in Bund und Ländern [Higher education law in the federal and state governments], Werkstand: 53. Ergänzungslieferung Juli 2020*. [11]

KMK (2001), *Sachstands- und Problembericht zur „Wahrnehmung wissenschaftlicher Weiterbildung an Hochschulen"*. [9]

Maunz/Dürig (ed.) (2019), *Grundgesetz, Werkstand: 88. Ergänzungslieferung August 2019*. [10]

Nedelkoska, L. and G. Quintini (2018), "Automation, skills use and training", *OECD Social, Employment and Migration Working Papers*, No. 202, OECD Publishing, Paris, https://dx.doi.org/10.1787/2e2f4eea-en. [3]

OECD (2021), *Continuing Education and Training in Germany*, Getting Skills Right, OECD Publishing, Paris, https://dx.doi.org/10.1787/1f552468-en. [6]

OECD (2021), *Deutschland braucht ein kohärenteres Weiterbildungssystem, das die Bedürfnisse Geringqualifizierter besser berücksichtigt, Press release*, https://www.oecd.org/berlin/presse/deutschland-braucht-ein-kohaerenteres-weiterbildungssystem-das-die-beduerfnisse-geringqualifizierter-besser-beruecksichtigt.htm#:~:text=Deutschland%20braucht%20ein%20koh%C3%A4renteres%20Weiterbildungssystem,insgesamt%20s. [7]

OECD (2021), *OECD Skills Outlook 2021: Learning for Life*, OECD Publishing, Paris, https://dx.doi.org/10.1787/0ae365b4-en. [4]

Statistik Berlin-Brandenburg (2021), *Bevölkerungsvorausberechnung für das Land Brandenburg 2020-2030*. [1]

VGH Baden-Württemberg (2016), *Judgement of 11.12.2015 - 4 S 1652/15*, BeckRS. [13]

Wehling, G. (ed.) (2020), *Das Europalexikon (3.Auflage)*, Verlag J. H. W. Dietz Nachf. GmbH. [14]

Wissenschaftsrat (2019), *Empfehlungen zu hochschulischer Weiterbildung als Teil des lebenslangen Lernens*, Wissenschaftsrat, https://www.wissenschaftsrat.de/download/2019/7515-19.pdf?__blob=publicationFile&v=1. [5]

Notes

[1] § 2 Abs. 1, S. 1 *Hochschulrahmengesetz*.

[2] On the function of the freedom of the sciences, Art. 5(3) marginal 15 ff; on the freedom of the sciences as a warranty of obligation ("*Gewährleistungsgarantie*"), see marginal 195 ff.

[3] See, for instance, § 4(1) *Berliner Hochschulgesetz* (BerlHG), § 3(1) *Hamburgisches Hochschulgesetz* (HmbHG), § 3(1) *Hochschulgesetz Nordrhein-Westfalen* (HG NRW), § 2(1) *Landeshochschulgesetz Baden-Württemberg* (LHG BaWü).

[4] Art. 5(3) marginals 35 ff., 47 ff.

[5] See § 58 HRG, marginal 14 ff.

[6] According to the case law of Federal Constitutional Court (BVerfG), the primacy of European law is effective only by virtue of and within the framework of a continued authorization under constitutional law, so that substance of the basic protections of the German law can be maintained via the Federal Constitutional Court. See BVerfG, Judgment of 30.06.2009 – 2 BvE 2/08 u.a., NJW 2009, 2267, 2273, 2284, Rn. 240, 331. Insofar as the organs of the European Union act beyond their powers (ultra-vires), the primacy of European law does not apply, see BVerfG, Judgment of 05.05.2020 – 2 BvR 859/15 u.a., NJW 2020, 1647, 1669, Rn. 234.

[7] See Art. 4 TEU marginal 101.

[8] The federal government retains legislative power over admission to higher education and degrees awarded by HEIs only within concurrent legislations, Art. 73(2)(33) GG. Due to the divergence of legislation in the *Länder* (1st sentence, no. 6 of Art. 72(3)GG), this is of no substantial importance.

[9] In the version of the published version of 19 January 1999 (BGBl. I p. 18), as amended by Article 2 of the Act of 12 April 2007 (BGBl. I p 506).

[10] See marginal 8 ff.

[11] See marginal 10 ff

[12] Check BeckRS 2016, 40955, marginal 5.

[13] See § 5 HRG, marginal 20 ff.

[14] As permitted by the provisions of e.g. § 40(1) BerlHG, § 71(1) NRWHG, § 77(1) HmbHG, § 41(1) LHG BaWü.

[15] The focus areas of the working group on VET and continuing (vocational) education and training were i) ensuring the use of modern learning technologies in VET and CVET; ii) promoting proactive and flexible VET systems to support smart specialisation strategies and co-operation through industry clusters; iii) promoting quality and excellence in VET; iv) enhancing governance and funding through cost-sharing and investment in infrastructure; v) promoting learning mobility in VET, career paths without borders and the internationalisation of VET.

2 Legal analysis of the regulation of state aid in the EU

This chapter lays out the legal framework of the European Union (EU) for regulating state aid. It explains the rationale for the prohibition of state subsidies for programmes that have the potential to distort free trade in the single European market. It defines the terms used in the regulatory instruments and identifies what lawyers look for in analysing a particular activity to check its compliance with the law. It also describes the penalties that can be applied if an activity has received a state subsidy contrary to the terms of the European law on state aid. Given the variety of the forms of economic activity in the EU and the complexity of the law, exceptions to and exemptions from the rules have arisen; this has added to the complexity of the law.

The purpose and defining conditions of the prohibition on state aid

The legal provisions on state aid in the European Union (EU) are part of the competition rules in the third part of the Treaty on the Functioning of the European Union (TFEU). They are set out in Articles 107 to 109 TFEU. Their aim is to prevent distortion of competition within the European market that may arise as a result of preferential treatment given by Member States to undertakings (i.e. businesses) located on their territory (Wallenberg/Schütte, 2016[1])[1]. On this basis, Art. 107(1) TFEU prohibits state aid as a matter of principle. There are, however, exceptions. The rationale for making exceptions is that EU legislators are aware that it is impossible to enforce the ban strictly. While state subsidy for undertakings will, in principle, always distort a free market, there are occasions when market failure or market conditions justify paying a subsidy.

The fundamental prohibition of EU state aid is set out in Article 107(1) TFEU which states that:

> "any aid granted by a Member State or through State resources in any form whatsoever which distorts or threatens to distort competition by favouring certain undertakings or the production of certain goods shall, in so far as it affects trade between Member States, be incompatible with the internal market." (EC, 2009[2])

State aid is therefore deemed to have been granted if the following four defining characteristics are present:

- it is a measure undertaken by a Member State;
- the measure constitutes advantage/favourable treatment;
- of a specific undertaking (that is, it is selective);
- it thereby leads to the occurrence of (or, at least, the potential for) distortion of competition and impairment of inter-Community trade (Callies/Ruffert, 2016[3]) (Bartosch, 2016[4])[2].

This chapter elaborates on the defining conditions of the prohibition on state aid.

Defining conditions of the prohibition on state aid

Funding from state resources

The prohibition in Art. 107(1) TFEU distinguishes between aid granted by the state on the one hand and aid granted through state resources on the other. According to the established case law of the European Court of Justice (ECJ), this distinction serves to:

> "include in the concept of aid not only aid granted directly by the State but also aid granted by public or private bodies designated or established by the State" (ECJ, 1978[5]) (ECJ, 1982[6]) (ECJ, 1993[7])[3].

According to ECJ case law, there are two prerequisites for the existence of this condition: the state origin of the means used for the aid on the one hand, and the imputability to the state of these means on the other. These conditions must be fulfilled cumulatively (ECJ, 2002[8]).[4]

According to the ECJ's definition, state resources are therefore *"all the financial means by which the public authorities may actually support undertakings, irrespective of whether or not those means are permanent assets of the public sector"* (ECJ, 2002[8]).[5] Therefore, state resources according to Art. 107 (1) TFEU can include, in addition to resources of the *Länder* and the regional authorities, also resources of state-owned undertakings (for instance, public HEIs).

The legal status of the institution responsible for granting the funds is therefore irrelevant. However, a prerequisite for qualification as a state measure is that the measure is *imputable to the State*. This does not derive solely from the fact that the institution is state-owned. It is also not sufficient that the State controls the institution or can exercise a dominant influence. Rather, state influence or state control over the granting of funds must be concretely demonstrated (Wallenberg/Schütte, 2016[1])[6]. Indicators are sufficient for this purpose (EC, 2016[9]).[7] According to the ECJ judgment in the Stardust Marine case (ECJ, 2002[10]), for example, the factors to be examined are, in particular, the integration of the undertaking into the structures of the public administration; the nature of its activities and the exercise of them in normal competition with private operators; the legal status of the undertaking (i.e. whether it is governed by public law or general company law); the intensity of the supervision exercised by the public authorities over the management of the undertaking; and any other indicators showing, in the particular case, an involvement by the public authorities (or the unlikelihood of its non-involvement) in the adoption of a measure, having regard also to its scope, content or conditions. Case law sets high standards for the exclusion of imputability and tends towards a *de facto* presumption of imputability (Koenig/Förtsch, 2018[11]).[8]

This means, in principle, that funds for Brandenburg's HEIs may also be state funds.

Favour

The term "favour" under EU state aid law is much broader than the term "subsidy" (*subvention*) common in German law. A "favour" is understood to be not only positive benefits (such as subsidies), but any economic advantage, without adequate payment, which an undertaking would not have received under normal market conditions (i.e. without the intervention of the State) (ECJ, 1961[12]) (EuGH, 1994[13])[9]. These can be positive benefits or relief from burdens and charges that the undertaking would normally have to bear. The defining character is, therefore, to be understood as *any granting of an economic advantage without appropriate (or fair market) consideration*. Typical examples are: non-recoverable subsidies, low-interest or interest-free loans, the assumption of guarantees and the transfer of land or buildings.

In order to assess the central criterion of the appropriateness (*Marktüblichkeit*) of the favour, both ECJ and the European Commission (EC) have consistently applied the "private investor test", which compares the investment behaviour of the public sector with that of a hypothetical private market participant (ECJ, 1996[14]) (ECJ, 1999[15]) (EGC, 1991[16])[10]. Whether an economic favour is to be regarded as appropriate or inappropriate for the market is assessed according to whether a private investor acting economically in the role of the public authority would have carried out or would carry out a comparable measure in favour of the respective undertaking.

Selectivity

The defining character of state aid also presupposes that the measures confer an advantage on one particular undertaking or production sector over others, i.e. that they have a *selective* effect. The selectivity requirement is intended, in particular, to exclude from the scope of EU state aid rules such as the general economic policy measures of a Member State which benefit everyone and therefore do not favour one undertaking over another in competition (Bartosch, 2016[4])[11].

Distortion of competition and impairment of inter-State trade

However, a favour in the sense of EU state aid rules is only deemed to have come into existence if it leads (or, at least, has the potential to lead) to a distortion of competition. Aid (in the sense of a selective grant through state resources) distorts competition only if that aid improves the position of the beneficiary or a third party in the applicable market *to the detriment of* their (potential) competitors. In order to determine whether this applies, it is necessary to compare the competitive situation before and after an (intended) subsidy is compared (ECJ, 1974[17]) (ECJ, 1980[18])[12].

Ultimately, a measure must also affect trade between Member States in order to be covered by the prohibition rule of Article 107(1) TFEU. Trade in the sense of this requirement is to be understood as the entire trade in goods and services between Member States. An effect on trade exists if the state measure in question has an impact of some kind on trade between Member States or throughout the Union (ECJ, 1999[19]) (ECJ, 1994[20]) (ECJ, 1991[21]) (ECJ, 1988[22]).[13]

The meaning of the term "undertaking"

The EU ban on state aid set out in Art. 107(1) TFEU presupposes that certain undertakings or branches of production are favoured. The term "undertaking" is particularly important in the assessment of CET at HEIs under EU state aid law. The term "undertaking" is a functional concept; it applies to any entity engaged in an economic activity, regardless of its legal form or financing. Thus, it is possible that a unit – in this case a HEI – is not an "undertaking" with regard to one activity, (such as delivery of undergraduate degree programmes, which is not seen as an economic activity) but can be an "undertaking" with regard to another activity, such as contract research (which is an economic activity). Consequently, it is not the HEI that is to be regarded as a unit, but its individual activities.

Case law considers an economic activity to be "any activity consisting in offering goods and services in a given market" (ECJ, 2006[23]).[14] A market connection is generally to be affirmed if the activity in question is not a purely sovereign activity and can, in principle, also be performed by a private undertaking. The intention to make a profit is not required for the activity to be deemed economic (ECJ, 2004[24]) (EGC, 2004[25]).[15]

The levels of EU rules on state aid

The notion of an undertaking therefore assumes economic activity. Every state-supported activity in the area of higher education must be considered on two levels of EU state aid law, as detailed in Figure 2.1, when deciding whether it is classified as economic or non-economic. It should be noted that a functional approach is decisive as even within an undertaking one area of activity can be economic while another is non-economic.

Figure 2.1. Levels of state aid under EU law – the example of HEI activities

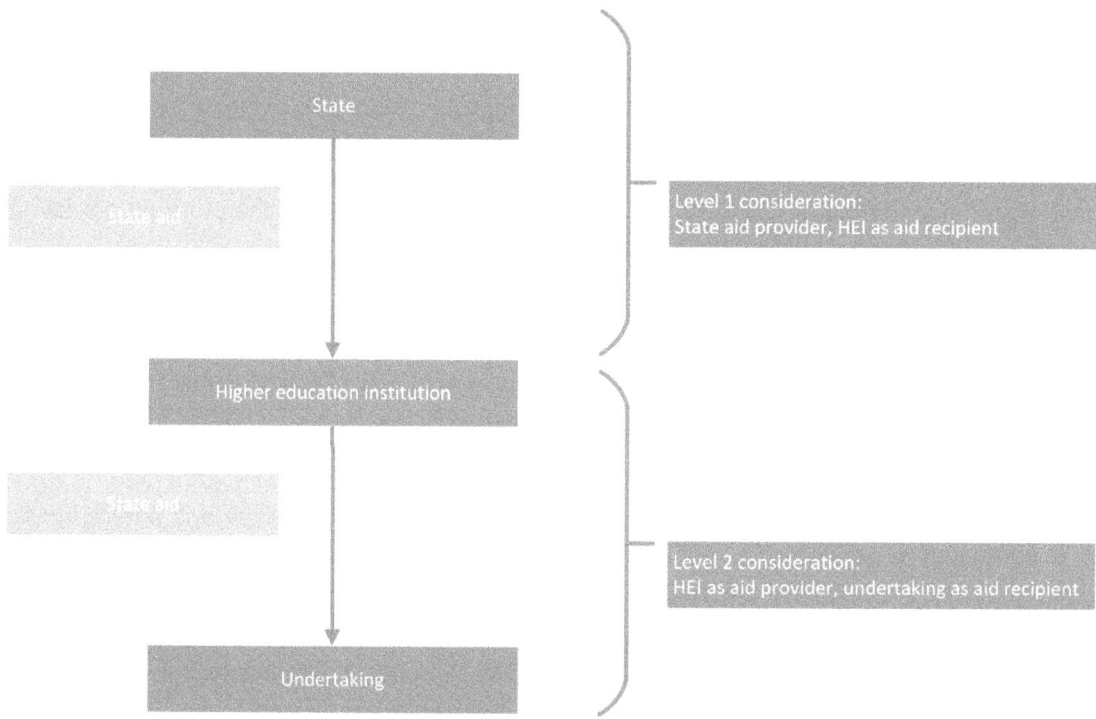

Level 1 concerns the funding of the HEI by the government (either federal or a *Land*). HEIs can also carry out economic activities within the meaning of EU state aid law. That means that they then compete with other, private undertakings and, as a consequence, they are then treated as *undertakings* within the meaning of EU state aid law. As an example: assuming that any CET programme was assessed as being an economic activity, the HEI would then be acting as an undertaking and, therefore, any funding for the programme in question granted through public resources would be incompatible with the EU state aid law and thus, subject to the EU prohibition on state aid. This is because the HEI would be receiving funds from the state which it could then use to offer its courses more cheaply than its competitors and would therefore have an economic advantage. This would apply *mutatis mutandi* to other economic activities such as funding equipment or laboratories that are rented to third parties, or funding infrastructure or personnel which or who are used to conduct contract research or to provide services to other undertakings (EC, 2016[9]).[16]

Level 2 concerns indirect state aid. If a publicly financed HEI allows a private party to participate indirectly in its state funding, then that private party is seen to have been granted state aid. An example of indirect state aid of this kind arises if a HEI provides services funded by the state to a company without appropriate consideration. The regulation of indirect aid is intended to ensure that state funding of HEIs does not influence the market in a circuitous way and ultimately lead to a distortion of competition. With regard to CET at HEIs, this could be the case, for example, if a HEI as an "aid provider" passed on state funding to another undertaking as an "aid recipient" to provide services for CET programmes within a co-operation framework.

However, whether a state measure can be deemed to be at hand must be examined precisely in each individual case. It does not automatically follow from the fact that services are provided by the public HEI for the benefit of a private third party. Rather, the "Stardust Marine" criteria set by the ECJ must always be taken into account when attributing benefits to the state.

Exclusions and exceptions

The fulfilment of the defining conditions for EU state aid in Art. 107(1) TFEU generally results in the incompatibility (and therefore, the prohibition) of state aid. There are two types of exceptions to this prohibition. One is that an exclusion in the form of a **general exemption** can apply to the specific measure. The other is that the measure can be justified on the basis of a **justifying exception** to this prohibition granted by the EC. The consequences are the same: In both cases, the obligation to *notify* the measure to and *obtain approval* from the EC pursuant to the first sentence of Article 108(3) TFEU does not apply (notification and approval together constitute the "notification procedure"). Therefore, the state funds may be applied to the activity without a notification procedure.

Exemptions under EU state aid rules can be found in particular in the *De Minimis* Regulation (EU) No 1407/2013 (EC, 2013[26])[17] and the General Block Exemption Regulation (EU) No 651/2014[18] (GBER) (EC, 2014[27]). The General Block Exemption Regulation (GBER) contains special exemptions for research and development (Art. 25 *et ff*. GBER). In addition, measures in favour of undertakings providing "services of general economic interest" may be exempted from the EU ban on state aid. This exemption is based on the Altmark Trans Judgment of the ECJ and the Almunia exemption decision by the EC (EC, 2012[28]).[19] This decision is part of the Almunia package. It requires that the undertakings in question, as beneficiaries of the aid, must have been "entrusted" by the aid provider with the provision of these services. The application of these (and other possible) exemptions to the provision of CET in higher education is elaborated in Chapter 3 below.

If a state measure fulfils the defining criteria for EU state aid and no possibilities for exemption apply, the measure must be notified to the EC following a notification procedure. The EC then examines whether the measure constitutes state aid and whether it can be approved on the basis of the exceptions under Article 107(2) and (3) TFEU or on the basis of special regulations.

Consequences of incompatibility of aid

The consequences of receiving state benefits that are found to be incompatible with EU state aid rules can be severe. This is particularly true for publically funded HEIs. The granting and receipt of illegal subsidies can – if discovered – have negative consequences for the beneficiary at both EU and national levels.

If a state measure meets the criteria for EU state aid and there is no exemption or approval by the EC, there is a risk – at **the EU level** – that the EC will conduct a formal state aid investigation. The EC could become aware of the facts either on its own initiative – through reports in the press or through a publicly conducted discussion in political decision-making bodies –or as a result of a complaint by competitors of the aid recipient. If the EC concludes that incompatible aid has been granted, it orders the recovery of the aid by the granting Member State. The recovery order is retroactive; it covers the ten years preceding the decision of the EC. In the recovery order, the EC usually includes interest on the aid amount for the entire period for which it was received.

At **the national level**, the Federal Court of Justice (*Bundesgerichtshof*, BGH) has clarified in established case law that all legal acts underlying the incompatible granting of aid are void from the outset. This has the consequence that the acts underlying the aid – such as, for example, grant notices to HEIs, or guarantee declarations – are invalid and must be reversed. This legal consequence ensues automatically. Competitors of the aid recipient can bring an action for a declaratory judgment before a regional court (*Landgericht*) or an administrative court (*Verwaltungsgericht*) to have the contractual or grant relationship declared null and void.[20]

The prohibition of cross subsidies and requirement for separate accounting under EU state aid rules

As noted above, one area of HEI activity may be economic while another is non-economic (ECJ, 2006[29]).[21] Therefore, it is necessary to prevent public funds that were intended for the **non-economic** activity of educational institutions from being used to subsidise **economic** activities. This is because cross-subsidisation can also constitute aid within the meaning of Article 107(1) TFEU and can therefore trigger legal consequences of incompatible aid.

According to Section 2.1.1. Point 18 of the R&D Framework of the EC, public funding of the non-economic activities of a research institution that carries out both economic and non-economic activities does not fall under the prohibition of state aid in Article 107 (1) TFEU:

> "if... the two kinds of activities and their costs, funding and revenues can be **clearly separated** so that cross-subsidisation of the economic activity is effectively avoided." (EC, 2014[30])[22]

Aid is deemed to be granted if the economic activity is financed with public funds from the non-economic activity. The prohibition of cross-subsidisation then applies. Therefore, to avoid incompatibility with state aid rules, it is necessary to be able to prove the absence of cross subsidy by maintaining separate accounts for the economic and non-economic activities, so that, in the words of the R&D Framework of the EC

This **requirement for the separation of accounts** means that all revenues and expenses must be clearly attributable. It must be possible to clearly separate non-economic and economic activities and their costs, financing and revenues. Only then is there no danger of cross-subsidisation of economic activities by non-economic activities.

However, the HEI must contend with the prohibition of cross-subsidisation only if it engages in economic activities at all and is considered an enterprise in relation to these activities. With regard to the compatibility of HEIs' CET offerings with EU state aid rules, it is therefore first necessary to classify them as economic or non-economic. This classification is discussed in the following chapter.

References

Bartosch (2016), *EU-Beihilfenrecht, 2. Auflage.* [4]

Callies/Ruffert (ed.) (2016), *TEU/TFEU, 5. Auflage 2016.* [3]

EC (2016), *Commission Notice on the notion of State aid as referred to in Article 107(1) of the Treaty on the Functioning of the European Union, OJ C 262 of 19.07.2016.* [9]

EC (2014), *Commission Regulation (EU) Nr. 651/2014 of 17.06.2014 declaring certain categories of aid compatible with the internal market in application of Articles 107 and 108 of the Treaty.* [27]

EC (2014), *Communication from the Commission – Framework for State aid for research and development and innovation, OJ C 198 of 27.06.2014.* [30]

EC (2013), *Commission Regulation (EU) No 1407/2013 of 18.12.2013 on the application of Articles 107 and 108 of the Treaty on the Functioning of the European Union to de minimis aid.* [26]

EC (2012), *Commission Decision of 20.12.2011 on the application of Article 106(2) of the Treaty on the Functioning of the European Union to State aid in the form of public service compensation granted to certain undertakings entrusted with the operation, 2012/21/EU.* [28]

EC (2009), *Core provisions of the Treaty on the Functioning of the European Union (TFEU)*, https://ec.europa.eu/competition/state_aid/legislation/compilation/a_01_03_11_en.pdf. [2]

ECJ (2006), *Judgment of 01.07.2006 – C-49/07*, BeckRS. [29]

ECJ (2006), *Judgment of 23.03.2006, C-237/04*, BeckRS. [23]

ECJ (2004), *Judgment of 16.03.2004 – C-264/01*, BeckRS. [24]

ECJ (2002), *Judgment of 16.05.2002 – C-482/99, EuZW 2002, 468.* [10]

ECJ (2002), *Judgment of 16.05.2002 – C-482/99, EuZW 2002, 468, 470.* [8]

ECJ (1999), *Judgment of 17.06.1999 – C-75/97*, BeckRS. [19]

ECJ (1999), *Judgment of 29.04.1999 – C-342/96*, BeckRS. [15]

ECJ (1996), *Judgment of 11.07.1996 – C-39/94*, BeckRS. [14]

ECJ (1994), *Judgment of 14.09.1994 – C-278/92*, BeckRS. [20]

ECJ (1993), *Judgment of 17.03.1993 – C-72/91.* [7]

ECJ (1991), *Judgment of 21.03.1991 – C-303/88*, BeckRS. [21]

ECJ (1988), *Judgment of 13.07.1988 –102/87*, BeckRS. [22]

ECJ (1982), *Judgment of 13.10.1982 – C-213/81.* [6]

ECJ (1980), *Judgment of 17.09.1980 – 730/79*, NJW. [18]

ECJ (1978), *Judgment of 24.01.1978 – 82/77.* [5]

ECJ (1974), *Judgment of 02.07.1974 – 173/73*, BeckRS. [17]

ECJ (1961), *Judgment of 23.02.1961 – 30/59, 72052*, BeckRS 2004. [12]

EGC (2004), *Judgment of 14.10.2004 – T-137/02*, BeckRS. [25]

EGC (1991), *Judgment of 21.01.1991 – T-129/95*, BeckRS. [16]

EuGH (1994), *Judgment of 15.03.1994 – C-387/92*, BeckRS 2004. [13]

Grabitz/Hilf/Nettesheim (ed.) (2016), *Das Recht der Europäischen Union, Werkstand: 59. Ergänzungslieferung Juli 2016*. [1]

Streinz (ed.) (2018), *EUV/AEUV, 3. Auflage 2018*. [11]

Notes

[1] See Art. 107 AEUV Rn. 10.

[2] See Bartosch, EU-Beihilfenrecht, 2. Auflage 2016, Art. 107 AEUV Rn. 1 ff.; Cremer in: Callies/Ruffert, EUV/AEUV, 5. Auflage 2016, Art. 107 Rn. 10 ff.

[3] ECJ, Judgment of 24.01.1978 – 82/77, marginal 23-25 in juris; ECJ, Judgment of 13.10.1982 – C-213/81, marginal 22 in juris; ECJ, Judgment of 17.03.1993 – C-72/91, marginal 19 in juris.

[4] ECJ, Judgment of 16.05.2002 – C-482/99, EuZW 2002, 468, 470, marginal 24.

[5] See marginal 37.

[6] See Art. 107 AEUV marginal 33.

[7] See p.10. marginal 41ff.

[8] See: Koenig/Förtsch in: Streinz, EUV/AEUV, 3. Auflage 2018, Art. 107 Rn. 62.

[9] ECJ, Judgment of 23.02.1961 – 30/59, BeckRS 2004, 72052; EuGH, Judgment of 15.03.1994 – C-387/92, BeckRS 2004, 76937, marginal 13.

[10] ECJ, Judgment of 11.07.1996 – C-39/94, BeckRS 2004, 76964, Rn. 60; Judgment of 29.04.1999 – C-342/96, BeckRS 2004, 76583, marginal 41; EGC, Judgment of 21.01.1991 – T-129/95 et al, BeckRS 1999, 55045, marginal 104 ff.

[11] Bartosch, EU-Beihilferecht, 3. Auflage 2020, Art. 107 AEUV, marginal 135.

[12] ECJ, Judgment of 02.07.1974 – 173/73, BeckRS 2004, 71968, marginal 36/40; Judgment of 17.09.1980 – 730/79, NJW 1981, 1152, 1152 f.

[13] See ECJ, Judgment of 17.06.1999 – C-75/97, EuZW 1999, 534, 537, marginal 47; Judgment of 14.09.1994 – C-278/92, BeckRS 2004, 75925, marginal 40; Judgment of 21.03.1991 – C-303/88, BeckRS 2012, 80903, marginal 27; Judgment of 13.07.1988 –102/87, BeckRS 2004, 70634, marginal 19.

[14] ECJ, Judgment of 23.03.2006, C-237/04, BeckRS 2006, 70228, marginal 28 f. with reference to Judgments of 23.04.1991 – C-41/90, NJW 1991, 2891, 2891f., maginal 21; Judgment of 21.09.1999 – C-67/96, marginal 7 – Albany; of 12.09.2000, adjunct marginals. C-180/98 to C-184/98, marginal 74 – Pavlov et al., and of 01.07.2006 – C-49/07, WuW 2008, 1129, 1130, marginal 22.

[15] ECJ, Judgment of 16.03.2004 – C-264/01, EuZW 2004, 241, 243, marginal 46; EGC, Judgment of 14.10.2004 – T-137/02, BeckRS 2004, 78076, marginal 50ff.

[16] See Commision Notice on the notion of State aid, OJ C 262 of 19.07.2016, p. 1 ff., marginal 218.

[17] Commission Regulation (EU) No 1407/2013 of 18.12.2013 on the application of Articles 107 and 108 of the Treaty on the Functioning of the European Union to de minimis aid, OJ L 352 of 24.12.2013, So 1.

[18] Commission Regulation (EU) Nr. 651/2014 of 17.06.2014 declaring certain categories of aid compatible with the internal market in application of Articles 107 and 108 of the Treaty, OJ. L 187 of 26.06.2014, p. 1.

[19] 2012/21/EU: Commission Decision of 20.12.2011 on the application of Article 106(2) of the Treaty on the Functioning of the European Union to State aid in the form of public service compensation granted to certain undertakings entrusted with the operation of services of general economic interest, OJ L 7 of 11.01.2012, p. 3.

[20] For examples of civil action for declaratory ruling on incompatible aid: BGH, Judgment of 12.10.2006 – III ZR 299/05, NVwZ 2007, 973; BGH, Judgment of 24.10.2003 – V ZR 48/03, EuZW 2004, 254; BGH, Rulling of 20.01.2004 – XI ZR 53/03, EuZW 2004, 252.

[21] See e.g ECJ, Judgment of 01.07.2006 – C-49/07, BeckRS 2008, 70730, marginal 25.

[22] Communication from the Commission – Framework for State aid for research and development and innovation, OJ C 198 of 27.06.2014, p. 1.

3 Classifying continuing education and training under EU state aid law

This chapter provides first an overview of the criteria for distinguishing between economic and non-economic activities. It discusses the notion of an "undertaking" in EU state aid law in relation to continuing education and training (CET) at public HEIs. It examines the relevant judgments by the European Court of Justice (ECJ), it looks at how the ECJ's decisions on education-related cases can inform the understanding of state aid rules, and it discusses how those judgments are represented in publications and decisions by the European Commission (EC). The interpretation of the distinction between economic and non-economic activities at HEIs in KMK Guidelines is also discussed. This chapter also elaborates on the exceptions to and exemptions from the rules on state aid and indicates how they apply to CET; and explains how the costs of a programme should be analysed and fees set to remain within the state aid rules.

Classification of CET as economic or non-economic

One of the reasons for the legal uncertainty surrounding CET is that the European Commission (EC) has not made a decision on continuing education and training (CET) in higher education. This means that it is necessary to analyse ECJ case law and EC decisions on related types of activity and to infer how they would interpret CET cases if they came for judgment. To do so, this analysis looks at ECJ case law and EC decisions that have parallels with CET, and discusses how programmes should be classified under EU law as "economic" (meaning they may not be subsidised) or "non-economic" (in which case, the prohibition on state subsidy will not apply). Beyond this initial classification sit other criteria and defining characteristics that are used in the assessment of the applicability of the state aid rules to a CET programme, leading to a set of criteria and principles that underpin the assessment of the applicability of the state aid law to CET.

The relevance of the "undertaking" notion in EU state aid rules for CET at public HEIs

As noted in Chapter 2, the distinction between non-economic and economic activities is decisive for the notion of an "undertaking" under EU state aid law. An "enterprise" is any entity engaged in an economic activity, regardless of its legal form and the way it is funded (ECJ, 1991[1]).[1] Therefore, having the status of an undertaking means that an entity is engaged in an **economic activity**. A HEI is not an enterprise in the sense of EU state aid law if, and to the extent that, it carries out non-economic activities. On the other hand, a HEI's economic activities should not be funded by the state. The funding of economic activities with state resources is subject to the prohibition of state aid.

CET does not belong to the core areas of sovereign activity, which are inherently non-economic (such as, for example, national defence, policing or the penal system) (Mestmäcker/Schweitzer, 2016[2]).[2] Therefore, classification depends on an examination of the nature of a CET programme, to determine how closely it meets the characteristics of an economic activity, by looking at four criteria:

- the existence of **private competition**;
- the **funding structure** and a corresponding profit motive;
- the embedding of the respective programme in the **state education system**;
- a possible **special state/public interest** in the specific programme.

The ECJ made a further clarification regarding the significance of competition, which is important for the evaluation of CET programmes offered by higher education institutions. The classification as an **economic activity** depends on whether the activity in question is carried out on a market in competition with other or potential economic agents (ECJ, 2006[3]).[3] Thus, if the offer by the entity in question competes with that of economic agents pursuing the same goal, this speaks in favour of its classification as an economic activity.[4] This is important in the present case, because CET programmes offered by state institutions of higher education can compete with those offered by private providers.

This suggests that CET at HEIs can, at least in principle, be either economic or non-economic, with, possibly, some CET programmes meeting the criteria for economic activities and some not.

The classification of CET as economic or non-economic is not straightforward because of the complexity of the criteria above and because of how they are understood in the complex, multi-layered legal system in the EU. Therefore, this chapter analyses the treatment of education in the legal system to identify the principles that are likely to guide the ECJ and the EC in their interpretation of the status of CET in Brandenburg's HEIs, before summarising how the four criteria apply in the case of higher education CET.

ECJ case law on the notion of services

EU treaties, regulations and directives do not include any explicit decisions on the classification of CET as economic or non-economic. However, ECJ has developed case law on services, (including education, and, in one case, CET). This case law is currently being codified by the EC – that is, translated – into EU state aid rules.

Development of case law on the notion of services

The ECJ has never directly ruled on the classification of CET under EU state aid rules. The question of the classification under EU law of educational programmes, especially CET programmes, has been raised several times in cases before the ECJ, but not specifically in connection with the prohibition of state aid in Art. 107(1) TFEU, but in relation to the notion of services in Art. 57 TFEU.

The **notion of services** is defined by the TFEU within the framework of the EU's fundamental freedoms. The freedom to provide services, in accordance with Art. 56 *et seq.* TFEU, is one of the fundamental freedoms that underpin the operation of the EU (as is, for example, the free movement of goods). These fundamental freedoms serve to establish the internal market within and between the EU Member States. According to Art. 57(1) TFEU, "services" within the meaning of the EU treaties are services which are normally provided for remuneration, insofar as they are subject to the provisions on the free movement of goods and capital and on the free movement of persons. According to ECJ case law, remuneration in this context constitutes the economic consideration for the service in question (ECJ, 1988[4]).[5]

Box 3.1 below sets out the ECJ judgments in the Humbel and Edel case (ECJ, 1988[4])[6], the Wirth case (ECJ, 1993[5])[7], the Schwarz and Gootjes-Schwarz case (ECJ, 2007[6])[8], the Zanotti case (ECJ, 2010[7])[9] and the Kirschstein case (ECJ, 2019[8]).[10] The essential parts of the reasoning of the judgments are first reproduced and then set in relation to each other.

Box 3.1. ECJ cases on education, considered as a service

The Humbel and Edel case

The first examination of educational services under the notion of services was carried out by the ECJ in the Humbel and Edel case. In this case, the parents of a French pupil brought an action because he had to pay an enrolment fee to attend secondary school in Belgium while Belgian pupils were not required to pay such a fee. The parents refused to pay the fee. One of the issues in this case was the classification of education at the Belgian secondary school as a service within the meaning of EU law. The ECJ denied the status as a service on the following grounds (ECJ, 1988[4]):

> *"The essential characteristic of remuneration thus lies in the fact that it constitutes consideration for the service in question, and is normally agreed upon between the provider and the recipient of the service.*
>
> *This characteristic is, however, absent in the case of courses provided under the national education system. First of all, the State, in establishing and maintaining such as system, is not seeking to engage in gainful activity but is fulfilling its duties towards its own population in the social, cultural and educational fields. Secondly, the system in question is, as a general rule, funded from the public purse and not by pupils or their parents.*
>
> *The nature of the activity is not affected by the fact that pupils or their parents must sometimes pay teaching or enrollment fees in order to make a certain contribution to the operating expenses of the system. A fortiori, the mere fact that foreign pupils alone are required to pay a minerval can have no such effect."*

The Wirth case

In the Wirth case, the ECJ had to rule again on the question of whether an educational programme should be classified as a service. In this case, the plaintiff, a German citizen, sought educational support from the German state under the Federal Training Assistance Act (BAFöG) to receive funding to study jazz saxophone in the Netherlands. However, he was denied BAFöG support. In its judgment, the ECJ denied the service character of the course of study in question (ECJ, 1993[5]), on the grounds:

> "As the Court has already emphasized [in the Humbel and Edel case], the essential characteristic of remuneration lies in the fact that it constitutes consideration for the service in question, and is normally agreed upon between the provider and the recipient of the service. In the same judgment, the Court considered that such a characteristic is absent in the case of courses provided under the national education system. First of all, the State, in establishing and maintaining such a system, is not seeking to engage in gainful activity, but is fulfilling its duties towards its own population in the social, cultural and educational fields. Secondly, the system in question is, as a general rule, funded from the public purse and not by pupils or their parents. The Court added that the nature of the activity is not affected by the fact that pupils or their parents must sometimes pay teaching or enrolment fees in order to make a certain contribution to the operating expenses of the system.
>
> Those considerations are equally applicable to courses given in an institute of higher education which is financed, essentially, out of public funds.
>
> However, as the United Kingdom has observed, whilst most establishments of higher education are financed in this way, some are nevertheless financed essentially out of private funds, in particular by students or their parents, and which seek to make an economic profit. When courses are given in such establishments, they become services within the meaning of Article 60 of the Treaty. Their aim is to offer a service for remuneration.
>
> However, the wording of the question submitted by the national court refers solely to the case where an educational institution is financed out of public funds and only receives tuition fees (Gebuehren) from the students.
>
> The answer to the first part of the first question must therefore be that courses given in an establishment of higher education which is financed essentially out of public funds do not constitute services within the meaning of Article 60 of the EEC Treaty."

The Schwarz and Goethes-Schwarz case

In the Schwarz and Goethes-Schwarz judgment, the ECJ developed its case law further. Here, the plaintiffs sought from the German tax authority tax benefits for the school fees they paid for their children's attendance at schools in other EU Member States. They argued that German income tax law provided only for these benefits for attendance at certain German private schools and that this was contrary to EU law. On the question of the classification of tuition offered by private schools as services, the ECJ judgment first summed up the two decisions mentioned above and added (ECJ, 2007[6]):

> "It is not necessary for that private financing to be provided principally by the pupils or their parents. According to consistent case-law, Article 50 EC does not require that the service be paid for by those for whom it is performed.
>
> The information from the referring court shows that the school fees paid by the Schwarzes to Cademuir School for the two children were estimated in themselves at DEM 10 000 per year at least. According to the German Government, that amount is significantly higher than that charged by private schools established in Germany and benefiting from Paragraph 10(1)(9) of the EStG.
>
> Since the decision to refer contains no precise information on the financing and operating methods of Cademuir School, it is in any event for the national court to assess whether that school is essentially financed by private funds."

The Zanotti case

Another ECJ judgment of particular interest for this study was handed down in the Zanotti case (ECJ, 2010[7]). This case directly concerned a CET programme. The dispute also revolved around a tax benefit under national (in this case, Italian) law, which an Italian lawyer did not receive. He had attended a master's course in international tax law at the International Tax Center in the Netherlands. The Italian tax authority refused to apply the national regulations to the case, according to which the amount charged by a corresponding state training institution could be deducted. On the question of whether the International Tax Center had provided services within the meaning prescribed by Union law, the court stated, with reference to the previous court decisions:

> "However, the Court has held that courses offered by educational establishments essentially financed by private funds, in particular by students and their parents, constitute services within the meaning of Article 50 EC, since the aim of those establishments is to offer a service for remuneration.
>
> Therefore, courses essentially financed by persons seeking training or professional specialisation must be regarded as constituting services within the meaning of Article 50 EC."

The Kirschstein case

Another case presented an opportunity to reconsider the previous case law. In the Kirschstein case (ECJ, 2019[8]), the ECJ was called upon to answer a number of questions referred for a preliminary ruling on whether services which are provided by a HEI fall within the definition of services in Art. 57 TFEU if they are offered by private institutions that act with the intention of making a profit. It is not so much the judgment itself that deserves special attention, but the opinion of Advocate General Bobek. In his submission, the Advocate General took the opportunity to subject the delimitation criteria of the case law to fresh examination[11]. He questioned the generalisation of their assessment. The strict boundary between state and private HEIs can no longer apply in today's higher education landscape, as even state-organised HEIs are increasingly moving into the realm of private-sector activity[12]. He therefore proposed to dissolve the distinction between private and public providers, proposing that parallels could be drawn with the health system (where both private and public providers are active in providing health care and whose services are classified as "non-economic services of general interest", to which the freedom to provide services does not apply. The Advocate General argued that it would make logical sense to differentiate in higher education law according to the activity and not according to the organisational ownership or structure. For this reason, the Advocate General proposed that the following criteria be used for differentiation.

According to Advocate General Bobek, a distinction should be made

- between each activity (and in particular each study programme);
- between level of education, as the social character of education was apparent only at primary and secondary level and not at the higher education level;
- according to the financing of the study programme and the question of consideration, whereby the following aspects played a role:
    - the assumption of costs (not exclusively and directly by the client); and
    - the nature of the market (the larger the market for a degree programme (national, European, global), the less it could be assumed that a special and unique social and cultural objective was being pursued).

However, the ECJ did not address these proposed criteria in its judgment, stating only with reference to previous case law:

> "It is also apparent from the Court's case-law that the organisation, for remuneration, of higher education services by institutions mainly financed by private funds and seeking to make a commercial profit, constitutes such an economic activity..."

Sources: ECJ (1988[4]), Judgment of 27.09.1988 – C-263/86, BeckRS 2004, 72754, marginal 17 ff; ECJ (1993[5]), Judgment of 07.12.1993 – C-109/92, BeckRS 2004, 74113, marginal 15 ff; ECJ (2007[6]), Judgment of 11.09.2007 – C-76/05, NJW 2008, 351, 353, marginal 41 ff; ECJ (2010[7]), Judgment of 20.05.2010 – C-56/09, IStR 2010, 487, 488, marginal 32 f; ECJ (2019[8]), Judgment of 04.07.2019 – C-393/17, GRUR 2019, 846; Opinion of Advocate General at ECJ (2018), 15.11.2018 – C-393/17, BeckRS 2018.

Summary of the criteria in ECJ case law

The judgments outlined in Box 3.1 indicate that the criteria established in the initial judgment (the Humbel and Edel case) remain decisive. Those criteria suggest that when education meets the following characteristics it will not be classified as a service for consideration:

- teaching provided within the framework of the **national education system**;
- **public funding** of the institution in question as an integral part of the education system, as opposed to funding essentially from private means (Kirschstein judgment), so that fees paid by students do not in themselves constitute private funding if they contribute only to a certain extent to maintaining the publicly-funded system;
- the **lack of profit motive** as opposed to a profit-oriented offer of courses (see Zanotti and Kirschstein judgments).

The public funding criterion was confirmed in the Wirth judgment. The court ruled that even a HEI funded from public resources but that received fees from the students did not provide them with a service. The characteristic of "public funding" did not therefore cease to exist simply because the students also had to pay fees.

In the Schwarz case, the ECJ ruled that the private financing of the educational institution was decisive for classifying the tuition offered as a service. This means that education provided by privately funded institutions can be regarded as services within the meaning of Art. 57 TFEU.

In the Zanotti judgment, the ECJ indicated that individual "courses" could be assessed with regard to the question of funding and not the institution as a whole. This would have the consequence that the private funding of an individual course could constitute a service. This would come close to the activity-based approach of EU state aid rules, which do not consider the entire organisation, but rather classify individual activities as economic or non-economic. However, the wording of the ECJ is too ambiguous to draw this conclusion with absolute certainty.

Had the ECJ adopted the Advocate General's argument in the Kirschstein case, it would have been necessary to differentiate between the individual activities of the HEI. In particular, the question would have arisen of whether paid-for CET at a HEI for people in employment constitutes an economic activity within the meaning of EU state aid rules, which would have had to be shown as such in the separate accounts required under EU state aid rules (see the discussion below about the need to separate the accounts). However, since the ECJ did not follow this line, the case law remains open in this respect.

Transferability of case law on the freedom to provide services to EU state aid rules

In principle, the case law on education as a service can also be applied to the classification of education activities as economic or non-economic.

The first argument in support of transferability is that both the freedom to provide services in Art. 57 *et seq.* TFEU and the prohibition of state aid in Art. 107(1) TFEU are designed to ensure the functioning of the internal market. Moreover, the notion of an "undertaking" within the meaning of Art. 107(1) TFEU presupposes the offering of goods or services (Callies/Ruffert, 2016[9]).[13] It is therefore reasonable to define the notion of service under EU state aid rules in the same way as the notion of service is defined under the freedom to provide services.

However, since the judgment in Humbel and Edel, the ECJ has focused on the funding of the *entire educational institution*. If the education *organisation*, as an entity, is funded by the state, the ECJ denies that the educational provision is a service. According to ECJ case law on competition law, on the other hand, the type of funding does not play a role in the definition of an enterprise under EU state aid rules (ECJ, 2006[10])[14]. Accordingly, an undertaking, within the meaning of EU state aid rules, could also exist even if a service within the meaning of Art. 57 TFEU is not offered.

Moreover, focusing on the funding of the entire HEI, as the ECJ does, contradicts the activity-based approach of EU state aid rules, which allows the notion that one entity could provide some economic activities and some non-economic activities. In the Zanotti decision, the ECJ at least hinted at the possibility of pursuing an activity-based approach if necessary.

Nevertheless, the EC itself assumes that the case law on services is transferable to EU state aid rules. This is expressed in its publications on EU state aid rules. As an example of this, in its Services of General Economic Interest (SGEI) Communication, the EC concludes (EC, 2012[11])[15]:

> "Case-law of the Union has established that education organised within the national educational system funded and supervised by the State may be considered as a **non-economic** activity."

The effect of that conclusion is that the EC has transferred the case law on the notion of services to the notion of (non-) economic activity under EU state aid rules.

The European Free Trade Association (EFTA) Court has also transferred the "Humbel criteria" of ECJ case law on the notion of services into its case law (which applies in the EFTA and the European Economic Area, EEA, States Norway, Iceland and Liechtenstein) (EFTA Court, 2008[12]).[16]

The ECJ has yet to hand down a clarifying decision on this issue. Therefore, there are very good reasons for applying in principle the criteria of case law to the assessment of CET programmes under EU state aid rules, in accordance with EC practice. However, these criteria are then to be applied to the individual CET programmes using the activity-related approach of EU state aid rules.

The role of the EC in classification

The classification of CET by the EC is particularly relevant for HEIs. This is because the EC is the supervisory authority that monitors compliance with competition and state aid rules and that sanctions violations[17]. EC practice as evidenced in its publications (Box 3.2) and in its decisions in its role as the state aid authority is discussed below (Box 3.3).

EC publications

EC publications are not binding legal acts to which the EC must adhere at all times. Nor are they independent, outward-looking legal acts of the EU and thus, they do not restrict the principles of "general" EU state aid law rules. Similar to national administrative regulations, however, they serve as a means of assessing the EC's state aid practice.

The publications discussed in Box 3.2 contain rules of interpretation and application, in particular on the question of which HEIs activities are not economic and therefore eligible for state support. In addition, they provide guidance on how state subsidies for economic activities of universities can be agreed. In this way, the publications give the most up-to-date overall view of the principles that the EC intends to follow.

Box 3.2. Decisions of the EC on the economic or non-economic classification of education

SGEI Communication

The SGEI Communication contains comments on how educational services can be classified as economic or non-economic. As noted above, referring to the ECJ case law on the notion of services, the EC states that "the EU has established that education funded and supervised by the State within a national education system may be considered as a non-economic activity" (EC, 2012[11]).[18]

Explaining the distinction between economic and non-economic activities, the EC continues:

> "Such public provision of educational services must be distinguished from services financed predominantly by parents or pupils or commercial revenues. For example, commercial enterprises offering higher education financed entirely by students clearly fall within the latter category. In certain Member States, public institutions can also offer educational services which, due to their nature, financing structure and the existence of competing private organisations, are to be regarded as economic." (EC, 2012[11]).[19]

R&D Framework

When interpreting and applying EU state aid rules in the field of research and teaching, the EC's framework for state aid for research and development and innovation (R&D Framework) contains criteria for distinguishing between economic and non-economic activities. In the R&D Framework, the EC defines the conditions and exceptions under which HEIs' research activities may be financed with public funds without violating the prohibition of state aid in Art. 107 TFEU. It sets out the conditions under which EU Member States and public institutions may fund undertakings to carry out research, development and innovation in a way that complies with state aid rules. It also sets out the rules under which the EC examines state aid notified to it. The Framework also clarifies that certain activities carried out by HEIs and research organisations do not fall within the scope of the state aid rules.

With regard to the classification of activities of HEIs, the R&D Framework states that it generally considers **primary activities** of research institutions and infrastructures as non-economic activities. This includes, in particular:

> "education for more and better skilled human resources. In line with ...[the Humbel judgment] and decisional practice of the EC, and as explained in the Notice on the notion of State aid and the SGEI Communication, public education organised within the national educational system, predominantly or entirely funded by the State and supervised by the State is considered as a non-economic activity." (EC, 2014[13]).[20]

EC notice on the notion of state aid

A further aid to interpretation is the EC's Notice on the notion of state aid (EC, 2016[14])[21]. In it, the EC explains explicitly which activities it believes can be seen as economic and which as non-economic. Many of the formulations can be found in the R&D Framework.

First, the EC explains its view in general terms with reference to ECJ case law:

> "Public education organised within the national educational system funded and supervised by the State may be considered as a non-economic activity. The Court of Justice held that the State: 'by establishing and maintaining such a system of public education and financed entirely or mainly by public funds and not by pupils or their parents [...] does not intend to become involved in activities for remuneration, but carries out its task towards its population in the social, cultural and educational areas." (EC, 2016[14]).[22]

The EC then emphasises that a proportionate financing through tuition or enrolment fees in the event of predominantly state funding does not change the classification as a non-economic activity:

> "The non-economic nature of public education is in principle not affected by the fact that pupils or their parents sometimes have to pay tuition or enrolment fees which contribute to the operating expenses of the system. Such financial contributions often only cover a fraction of the true costs of the service and can thus not be considered as remuneration for the service provided. They therefore do not alter the non-economic nature of a general education service predominantly funded by the public purse. These principles can cover public educational services such as vocational training, private and public primary schools, and kindergartens, secondary teaching activities in universities and the provision of education in universities."

The EC then explains that, conversely, substantial funding by parents or pupils, or from commercial sources, constitutes an economic activity:

> "Such public education services must be distinguished from services financed predominantly by parents or pupils or commercial revenues. For example, higher education financed entirely by students clearly falls within the latter category. In certain Member States, public entities can also offer educational services which, due to their nature, financing structure and the existence of competing private organisations, are to be regarded as economic."

In light of these principles, the EC lists activities that should not fall within the scope of the state aid rules. In this respect, the R&D Framework restates the following:

> "...the EC considers that certain activities of universities and research organisations fall outside the scope of the State aid rules. This concerns their primary activities, namely:
>
> education for more and better skilled human resources;
>
> the conduct of independent research and development for more knowledge and better understanding, including collaborative research and development;
>
> the dissemination of research results."

Sources: EC (2012[11]), Communication from the Commission on the application of the European Union State aid rules to compensation granted for the provision of services of general economic interest (footnote 101); EC (2014[13]), Communication from the Commission on Framework for State aid for research and development and innovation, 198/01, marginal 19(a), 2014/C 198/01; EC (2016[14]), Commission Notice on the notion of State aid as referred to in Article 107(1) of the Treaty on the Functioning of the European Union, OJ C 262 of 19.07.2016.

Summary of criteria in EC publications

The assessment of the three EC publications presented in Box 3.2 shows that ECJ case law on the notion of services has been transferred by the EC to EU state aid rules. However, the EC makes additions and its own assessments. However, it should be noted that CET at HEIs is not explicitly mentioned, and consequently, policy makers and higher education institutions still face considerable uncertainty regarding the application of the law.

In the view of the EC, "education and training" at HEIs can, in principle, be of a non-economic nature. This ruling is based on the education and training being, firstly, predominantly or completely funded by the state and, secondly, supervised by the state. This privilege does not necessarily apply to other HEI activities. However, in the R&D Framework, the EC identifies certain primary activities of HEIs as generally non-economic.

One such primary activity of higher education is "education for more and better skilled human resources". However, it is questionable whether this also includes CET at HEIs or, whether, by dint of the use of the word education and training ("*Ausbildung*" in the German text), only includes a person's initial (vocational) qualification (excluding subsequent upskilling). As a result, the open wording does not give a clear indication of whether the EC sees CET also as a primary activity of HEIs. However, the German wording

"*Ausbildung von mehr und besser qualifizierten Humanressourcen*" (education and training for better qualified human resources) suggests the possibility of the inclusion of CET.

If CET cannot be confidently categorised under "education and training for more and better skilled human resources", it is necessary to clarify the defining criteria to reach greater certainty as to the status of CET under the law. The EC refers to the case law, in other words, the type of funding, the intention to make a profit and the embedding in the state education system, but it is clear that the EC considers other criteria to be applicable as well. The EC's assessment refers to the "nature, financing structure and the existence of competing private organisations" of the educational services. Thus, the very existence of competing private organisations could also be taken as evidence of an economic activity. This is consistent with ECJ case law, according to which, for economic activities in general, it is also important whether the service in question competes with that of other economic operators. It remains open, however, whether the EC considers private competition to be a **sufficient** condition to constitute an economic activity, even if the CET programme is part of the public education system and is also publicly financed.

In particular, the primary activities of higher education according to the R&D Framework cannot be used directly for the classification of CET; CET is not among the examples given in the Framework. The common factor that differentiates non-economic activities from the economic activities mentioned is that they are recognisably part of the primary tasks of HEIs and are provided independently of the wishes of third parties. They are non-economic even if, as in the case of the privileged activity of knowledge transfer, fees are also charged, as long as such fees flow back into the non-economic domain.

Activities which, on the other hand, are performed in dependence on and targeted at the interests of third parties are considered to be of an economic nature, such as the contract research referred to in the R&D Framework.

Looking at the CET provided by HEIs, the decisive factor from the perspective of the EC is whether the CET offered is a *primary activity* of the HEI. The more clearly the CET programme can be derived from a specific educational mandate, the more likely it is to be classified as a non-economic activity. This also corresponds with the ECJ's formulation that educational programmes "within the framework of the state education system" are not services. However, it is not yet possible to definitively classify CET as such.

When considering the objective of EU state aid rules, the EC's adoption of funding predominantly from the public purse as a fundamental criterion in state aid rules can easily be criticised as it attaches importance to an economic approach that is linked to the type of **service** offered. In contrast, the rules do not give weight to the type and manner of **funding**.

The EC adopts an economically oriented approach, a "refined economic approach"[23], to its assessment of an activity against the state aid rules (EC, 2005[15]) (EC, 2009[16]) (EC, 2009[17]). This stance reflects the purpose of EU state aid rules and their objective to prevent distortions of competition within the internal market and impairment of trade between Member States (Bartosch, 2016[18])[24]. Whether or not there is a distortion of competition can ultimately only be answered if the competitive conditions on the market in question and their respective economic effects are taken into account.

The ECJ also takes an economic approach in its case law. According to the Court, the question to be examined under EU state aid rules is whether, in the context of a particular statutory scheme, a state measure is such as: "to favour 'certain undertakings or the production of certain goods' within the meaning of Article 92(1) of the Treaty in comparison with other undertakings which are in a legal and factual situation that is comparable in the light of the objective pursued by the measure in question". (ECJ, 2001[19]) (ECJ, 2005[20]).[25]

The substantial characteristics of EU state aid are to be interpreted on the basis of the objectives of EU state aid rules and the understanding described above.

The functional notion of an undertaking under EU state aid rules also shows that EU state aid rules are based on an economic approach. The question of whether an organisation qualifies as an undertaking is based solely on the pursuit of economic activity and not on the legal form, funding or profit orientation of the organisation. The question of whether a favour exists is also to be answered by means of an economic approach (Mederer, 2015[21]).[26]

Thus, the focus of the state aid assessment is on the economic nature of activities, and not on whether an activity is funded by the state. This is because EU state aid rules aim to prevent state funding causing distortions of economic activities. If the state funds an activity and if the fact of state funding were to result in a classification of the activity as non-economic, then that activity would be removed from the scope of EU state aid rules. The very thing that EU state aid rules intend to prevent would in fact lead to the activity being withdrawn from the scope of EU state aid rules through state financing. The consequence would be that EU state rules would fail to achieve their purpose.

Despite this contradiction, the EC has adopted funding structure as one of the criteria for assessment against EU state aid rules. In light of this clear EC policy, it should be applied accordingly in higher education, notwithstanding the doubts and risks outlined here, until such time as the issue is clarified by the EC or by the ECJ.

Decision-making practice of the EC with regard to state aid rules

Special attention must also be paid to the EC's decision-making practice on the classification of CET programmes. It appears that the EC does not systematically apply the criteria discussed above in every case. It is also apparent that the EC attaches considerable importance to proximity to and integration in the state education system (see Box 3.3).

Box 3.3. Cases on the application of state aid rules to higher education decided by the EC

Prerov Logistics College, Czech Republic

The Prerov Logistics College case (EC, 2006[22]) concerned a Czech private HEI that received a subsidy from the Czech Republic. The college offered an accredited bachelor's degree programme. The HEI generated its own income through tuition fees and had its own financial resources in the form of investment. However, the exact funding structure was not disclosed in detail.

The EC decided that this private college was not an undertaking in the sense of EU state aid rules and was part of the state education system. The educational programmes offered, and the research, development and other activities conducted within the college's study programme were dependent the approval of the Czech Ministry of Education. The college was barred from engaging in other activities. In addition, any profits could only be reinvested in the college's activities. The distribution of earnings was not possible, and therefore the EC concluded there was no intention to make a profit, deciding that overall, the college was not engaged in any economic activities but pursued a role in the education system in the general interest of the public.

The EC, in contrast to case law on the notion of services, did not base its decision on the funding of the HEI, and the partial funding from private resources was not brought forward as an issue. The decisive criterion here was legal integration into the public education system, in conjunction with a lack of profit-making intent and the corresponding state supervision.

Private Foundation of the Liceu Conservatorium, Spain

In 2018, in the Private Foundation of the Liceu Conservatorium case (EC, 2018[23]), the EC decided that granting funds to a private HEI to implement a state-recognised bachelor's degree programme in music does not constitute state aid if the programme is part of the state education system. This decision depended on the level of integration into the state education system and the majority funding.

The EC reiterated that the decision also applied if the pupils or parents paid part (in fact around 35%) of the fees for the course, but not if the pupils or parents bore the majority of the costs. The striking aspect of this case was that the Member State funded less than 50% of the costs of the degree course. This meant that the bachelor's degree programme was not fully or predominantly funded from state resources, and the EC expressed clear doubts as to whether this did not constitute an undertaking within the meaning of Art. 107 TFEU.

However, the EC did not have to decide on this question because it considered the study programme to be a measure aimed at preserving culture and promoting cultural education within the meaning of Art. 53 TFEU. The EC thus considered the measure to be compatible with the prohibition of state aid.

Partium Knowledge Centre, Hungary

The EC's decision in the Partium Knowledge Centre case (EC, 2008[24]) also highlighted that the services provided by the publicly funded HEI in Hungary were partly free of charge, partly benefited individuals and not undertakings and, concerning research and development services, fell under the relevant examples of the R&D Framework for non-economic activities.

BBC Digital Curriculum

In its decision on the BBC Digital Curriculum (EC, 2003[25]), the EC emphasised that the existence of a market could constitute economic activity even if the service in question was offered free of charge in this market. This is in line with the particular importance that the ECJ also attaches to the competition criterion for the notion of an undertaking.

Sources: EC (2006[22]), EC Decision of 08.11.2006, State aid No N 54/2006; EC (2018[23]), EC decision of 08.11.2018, State aid. 43700 (2018/NN) / C(2018) 7215; EC (2008[24]), EC decision of 26.11.2008, State aid No N 343/2008; EC (2003), EC decision of 01.10.2003, State aid No N 37/2003.

The Prerov Logistics College decision could play a role in the shaping of CET at HEIs in Brandenburg as it could mean that the integration of a CET programme in the state education system is more important to the EC than the funding structure. However, such a conclusion cannot be drawn with absolute certainty – the facts of the case in this decision by the EC are not presented in sufficient detail.

Interpretation of EU state aid rules in the KMK Guidelines

The Standing Conference of the Ministers of Education and Cultural Affairs of the *Länder* in the Federal Republic of Germany (*Ständige Konferenz der Kultusminister der Länder in der Bundesrepublik Deutschland*, KMK) has published a set of guidelines for differentiating between economic and non-economic activities at HEIs (KMK, 2017[26]). The Guidelines are intended to assist HEIs in assessing their programmes, but, unlike the judgments of the ECJ and the decisions of the EC, these are only advisory and have no legal standing. They contain some indications regarding CET programmes.

When do the KMK Guidelines treat CET at HEIs as an economic activity?

The KMK Guidelines are intended to offer a first orientation for classifying and assessing state aid for research, development and innovation (RDI) in terms of the EU state aid rules. They are primarily aimed at HEIs as institutions for research and knowledge dissemination in the terms to Section 1.3(ee) of the

R&D Framework. The guidelines (KMK, 2017[26]) do not offer a proper classification of CET at HEIs in terms of EU state aid rules on the basis of the R&D Framework and refer to European Union law:

> "The basis for the distinction between economic and non-economic activity under state aid rules is solely [European] Union law. Other alternatives, such as the criterion of national taxability or the distinction between sovereign and non-sovereign tasks are not suitable as differentiation criteria, as they are not congruent Europe-wide and sovereign tasks are essentially defined nationally. There are also exceptions where services are to be assumed to be non-economic despite their taxability. Furthermore, the objectives of the European Union framework and national tax law are not congruent." (KMK, 2017[26]).

This statement is followed by a conclusion by the KMK that is important for the assessment of CET:

> "Whether an educational service is of an economic nature therefore depends not only on the structure of the funding of the offer but also on the profit-making intention of the provider and on how the education sector is organised in the Member State concerned and whether there is a specific public interest in the services offered. When assessing whether educational services offered by private HEIs and funded by fees are an economic activity, the integration of those services into the state education and control system must also be taken into account. Differences in the circumstances in the Member States can lead to different assessments." (KMK, 2017[26]).

By using the term "educational service" (*Bildungsdienstleistung*), the KMK indicates that it does not understand education and training (*Ausbildung*) as initial (vocational) training only, but interprets the term broadly. In this interpretation, it is fundamentally possible to classify CET as a non-economic activity. This represents a concretisation of the R&D Framework, which leaves open the question of whether "education and training [*Ausbildung*] for better qualified human resources" includes CET or whether the use of the term *Ausbildung* restricts it to initial (vocational) training.

Like the R&D Framework, the KMK Guidelines place an emphasis on the structure and funding by the state. Section 9 of the Guidelines lists case studies intended to serve as aids to interpretation for HEIs and which are important for implementation at HEIs. Undergraduate study programmes and consecutive master's programmes are assigned to the non-economic sphere, in accordance with case law of the ECJ, if they constitute organised public education within the national education system that is predominantly or completely funded and supervised by the state. Indicators for this are, for example, conformity with the higher education institution plans of the *Länder*, agreements on study programmes and the requirement for accreditation. This should apply even if the undergraduate programmes are part-time and funded by fees. The KMK Guidelines state:

> "The levying of fees does not preclude classification insofar as these fees merely contribute to covering operational costs (additional costs caused by special formats, e.g. events at weekends, in the evenings or at special venues)." (KMK, 2017[26]).

This mirrors the approach of the EC, which has ruled that partial funding of education from fees does not constitute an economic activity. This is particularly the case if the educational programmes in question are integrated in the state education system. However, the reference in the Guidelines to "operational costs" (as opposed to capital costs or, possibly, overhead costs) is not found in the R&D Framework and thus represents a further refinement.

With regard to postgraduate master's study programmes, the KMK makes a differentiation that is linked solely to the way in which they are funded. From the KMK's point of view, a postgraduate master's study programme is also to be classified as non-economic if the programme is predominantly publicly funded (requirement 1) and state-supervised (requirement 2). "Predominant" state funding is assumed if 50% of the full costs are borne by the state. Further grounds are:

> "In the event of predominant funding by the state, the programme is classified in the non-economic domain. This enables the promotion of CET (also subject- or target group-specific) in accordance with the educational policy ideas of the respective Land." (KMK, 2017[26]).

Conversely, a postgraduate master's programme should consistently be classified as economic if it is not predominantly funded by the state. According to the KMK, state supervision alone is not sufficient to classify a programme as non-economic. This principle of classifying continuing education programmes according to the way in which they are funded is maintained throughout the KMK Guidelines.

This differentiation is continued for further education and training *(Fortbildung)*, whereby it is noted that *Fortbildung* is non-economic if there is "a special state interest in [it] (e.g. teacher training)". The same applies to language courses, which are to be deemed non-economic if there is a special state interest in them and they are predominantly funded from the public purse.

The KMK thus introduces a further characteristic, namely, "special state interest", in addition to structure and funding. A special state interest is inherent some CET programmes. The classification of CET as non-economic can therefore be linked to its "proximity" to the state education system. This allows the conclusion that the evaluation also depends on whether the particular CET programme is to be evaluated as education *(Bildung)* within the framework of the state education system. This criterion reflects the analysis of ECJ case law (described above – see Box 3.1).

Language courses, on the other hand, are considered to be economic insofar as they are completely or predominantly liable to fees or charges. In the case of internal CET *(interne Weiterbildungsangebote)*, the differentiation is changed: If the CET is provided by HEI staff, it is non-economic, but if third parties are involved, it is economic. The KMK Guidelines do not provide any further rationale for this differentiation.

In summary, the KMK Guidelines aim to find a solution under which HEIs can classify (vocational) CET courses as non-economic. To do this, the KMK makes use of two main elements:

- Element 1: predominantly state funding of the programme;
- Element 2: special state interest in the programme offered by HEIs.

This interpretation is clearly influenced by ECJ case law on state education, which foregrounds the state education system with its state organisation and the state interest. The predominantly public funding is apparently to be understood as indicating the state character of the programme, thus making it possible to classify the programme in the non-economic domain.

Critical examination of the KMK Guidelines

The KMK Guidelines understandably play an important role in practice as they make it possible for HEIs to define manageable delimitations. This is necessary in the absence of more detailed case law or codification of the EU framework by the EC.

Nevertheless, there is no overlooking that fact that the KMK Guidelines have weaknesses. These are addressed below, and recommendations for further development of the Guidelines for the future are given as part of recommendations for action.

Substantial state funding

If substantial state funding is to be a defining criterion for non-economic activity, an EU state aid contradiction arises.

Currently, the KMK Guidelines and the R&D Framework make the level of funding the defining criterion for classifying an educational activity as economic or non-economic. It was noted above that making the level of state funding a decisive criterion seems, at first glance, to be contradictory: the more funding for an activity is drawn from the public purse, the less the activity is subject to EU state aid rules, which aim to prevent distortion of competition by state funding. The counter view is that predominant state funding suggests that a CET programme is particularly relevant for the public interest, and this is an expression of the principle that the public interest is important for the classification of CET programmes at HEIs under EU state aid rules.

The dynamic nature of EU law and the general tendency to greater economisation makes it possible that funding will become less important as a criterion (Marwedel, 2014[27]) in the future and that this would be used only as an indicator for the more general criteria of relevance for the public interest. This would mean that classifying CET as a non-economic activity would be possible even if it is (fully) funded from fees. The decisive factor seems to be, therefore, that the CET programme in question can be justified as being in the public interest. The increasing importance of CET in the EU, as discussed in Chapter 1 of this report, is also relevant in this context. However, this assessment does not yet satisfy the criteria of EU state aid rules.

Another factor may be that provision of funding for CET programmes and a "specific" state interest could also be the result of a lack of services offered by private participants in the market. Why else should the state fund CET programmes at public HEIs? The state is concerned with safeguarding the availability of services because there is a shortage (or absence) on the German market.

"Special state interest"

According to the KMK Guidelines, the existence of a "special public interest" (Section 8) is a condition for a CET programme at a HEI to be non-economic. The lack of precision in this criterion makes it difficult to apply.

The special public significance of education means that any activity undertaken by a HEI can probably be classified as being in the "state interest." Education and training, and CET specifically, is already an explicit objective of the EU and is anchored in Art. 166(2) TFEU and the Preamble of TFEU[27]. In addition, CET is of increasing importance to societies in the EU, and CET is anchored as a core function in [German] higher education laws. Whereas § 21 HRG (old version) stipulated that HEIs should develop and offer opportunities for CET, after the amendment in § 2(1) HRG and in agreement with the higher education laws of the *Länder* – **continuing education and training** is assigned as a core task for HEIs, alongside research and teaching. Brandenburg's higher education legislation refers to CET in § 25 BbgHG. That section of the law confirms the responsibility of HEIs to develop and offer continuing education studies in accordance with § 3(1) BbgHG.

Thus, acting in the state interest does not provide a clear criterion for distinguishing between economic and non-economic activity. However, the proximity of the respective CET programme to the state's educational mandate can be a determining factor for its classification as non-economic, especially in cases of doubt.

Overall assessment of the KMK Guidelines

In agreement with the EC, the KMK Guidelines emphasise, in particular, the financing structure of CET programmes. However, they also cite a "specific state interest" clearly as a defining criterion. For example, certain language courses (such as the programme offered by the German Academic Exchange Service (DAAD)) could be classified as non-economic due to the special state interest in them (KMK, 2017[26]). The upshot is that it is not possible to classify every example of CET as an economic or non-economic activity using the KMK Guidelines. This begs the question of whether the Guidelines could be adapted better to EU criteria and thus could offer HEIs greater legal security. This will be discussed in further detail in Chapter 5.

Assessment of CET against the classification criteria

Two conclusions can be drawn from the discussions above.

Firstly, the EC does not explicitly classify CET at HEIs as a non-economic activity. Although education and training of better qualified human resources is generally considered non-economic, it cannot be said with certainty whether CET also falls under this category.

Secondly, it follows that, in the absence of a clear classification, it is a matter of individual definition criteria. The ECJ case law and the EC's practice show which criteria the EC would most probably apply at present when classifying CET programmes. The wording of the SGEI Communication and the EC Notice on the notion of State aid states:

> "In certain Member States, public entities can also offer educational services which, due to their nature, financing structure and the existence of competing private organisations, are to be regarded as economic." (EC, 2016[14]).

The following therefore addresses the assessment of higher education CET against the four primary criteria set out at the beginning of this section:

- the existence of **private competition**;
- the **funding structure** and a corresponding profit motive;
- the embedding of the respective programme in the **state education system** ("nature" of the service);
- a possible **special state or public interest** in the specific programme.

The first three criteria do not need to apply jointly. Only one criterion might be relevant for a particular CET programme.

However, as these decisions by the ECJ and the EC refer primarily to education and training services in general, it is not possible to say with absolute certainty how the criteria would be interpreted in relation to CET services. In particular, the ranking of the criteria identified is still unclear.

Competing private organisations

The case law of the ECJ on the notion of an undertaking suggests that whether the programme is offered on the market in competition with other economic operators may be relevant for the classification of CET programmes offered by HEIs. A CET programme that is not (or does not have the potential to be) in competition with private organisations cannot be held to be distorting trade and therefore, has no significance under EU state aid rules, and so could be classified a non-economic activity. This is because the prevention of distortions of competition is an essential aim of EU state aid rules. Consequently, the EU institutions are likely to be inclined to attach particular importance to this criterion when classifying CET programmes (Marwedel, 2014[27]). The SGEI Communication and the EC's notice on the notion of state aid speak more precisely of the "existence of competing private organisations".

The ECJ has stressed that competition with other economic operators can give rise to economic activities even if the respective goods or services are offered without the intention of making a profit (ECJ, 2006[3])[28], underlining the weight that the ECJ gives to the competition criterion. It is therefore reasonable to expect that the EC would classify a CET service as economic if it competes with services offered by other economic operators in a relevant market within the meaning of EU competition rules (EC, 1997[28]) (Marwedel, 2014[27]).

Funding structure and intention to return a profit

A second important criterion is the funding structure of the CET programme. Funding that is (at least) substantially granted from public resources speaks to a non-economic activity (according to the ECJ in the Wirth case, see Box 3.1 above), although, in the absence of clear case law, the possibility of an economic character despite predominantly public funding cannot be excluded.

Neither the ECJ nor the EC specify what proportion of funding may be called substantial. In the literature on CET, it is argued that a state funding ratio of more than 50% of the full costs for a particular course is to be considered "substantial" in the sense of ECJ case law (Marwedel, 2014[27]). This argument is supported by the fact that, where there are only two possible sources of funding, the word "substantial" must be taken to mean "more than half of the total funding". Funding by the state amounting to no more than 50% would therefore not constitute substantial state funding.

However, the argument that the activity is non-economic could still be made on the basis that a CET programme is operated without the intention of making a profit; in other words, at least half of it is privately funded, but overall it only covers costs (Marwedel, 2014[27]). However, there is a level of legal risk in that case, as the ECJ has never clarified the relationship between the funding ratio and the intention to make a profit. The EC has taken up the lack of intention to profit as an argument for non-economic activity and has connected that feature with integration into the state education system. This makes clear that considering defining criteria in isolation from each other is problematic.

In line with the activity-based approach of EU state aid rules, the funding structure of *individual CET programmes* must be examined. ECJ case law on the notion of services (Box 3.1) primarily focuses on the fact that the national education system is usually funded from the state budget and the court refers to the educational institution as an entire organisation. However, the EC assumes, especially in the R&D Framework, that a distinction is drawn between individual activities for the purposes of EU state aid rules. Since the notion of an undertaking under state aid rules differentiates according to economic unit rather than legal form, this is to be complied with.

Integration in the state education system

Integration into the state education system is another criterion used in particular by the EC, which refers to the "nature" of the educational service (see Box 3.3 above).

In principle, the more integrated an educational service is in the state education system and its regulations, the more likely it is to be non-economic. This is clear in the EC's decision on the Prerov Logistics College case (EC, 2006[22]), which set out criteria in favour of that position. The issue at hand was the state's permission to act as a tertiary education institution and to offer a certain course of studies. The limited freedom of action to develop other activities was also of importance. With regard to CET at public higher education institutions, there are some arguments in favour of it being of a non-economic "nature". Public institutions, which are subject to state recognition and supervision, fulfil a state mandate for CET. In some cases, state degrees are awarded (master's degrees). In Brandenburg, for example, HEIs remain responsible for content and examinations even when they collaborate with non-university institutions (§ 25(4) BbgHG).

Special state/public interest

Finally, the criterion of public interest requires separate consideration. The KMK Guidelines explicitly reference public interest as a criterion, but neither the ECJ nor the EC mention it. However, integration into the state education system and substantial public funding are associated with the public interest of the Member State. This suggests the possibility that the special public interest in CET programmes will play a more important role in ECJ case law and the practice of the EC in the future.

The special public interest criterion is relatively imprecise, as noted in the discussion of the KMK Guidelines above. This is because education, especially CET, is in the public interest because of the demographic and technological change described in Chapter 1, which have led to political priority on upskilling/reskilling the workforce. If this criterion were to become a determining factor in EU state aid rules in the future, the scope for states to fund CET would be greatly expanded. However, it remains to be seen whether the EC will abandon the "solid" criterion of the financing structure.

Prioritising the criteria

The fact that there are four criteria means that, in some cases, the order of priority of the defining criteria will arise. It cannot be deduced with certainty from the publications and decisions of the EC whether public funding can also constitute a non-economic activity if the service in question is in competition with private organisations. The explicit objective of avoiding distortions of competition by means of EU state aid rules suggests that, in principle, public funding cannot constitute a non-economic activity if the publicly-funded offering is in competition with the services offered by private organisations. (Marwedel, 2014[27]) also notes this lack of clarity, writing that competition from private organisation is certainly the most important criterion but is not a criterion for exclusion:

> "If there is clear competition from private organisations, the EC could consider objecting to state subsidies for CET at HEIs even if the funding structure and the nature of the CET provision actually constitute a non-economic activity. In areas where comparable competing offers exist, it is therefore to be assumed in principle that the activity is economic. However, with strong counter-arguments regarding the funding structure and, if applicable, the nature of the educational service, the classification as a non-economic activity can still be justified in individual cases." (Marwedel, 2014[27]).

Further defining criteria in prohibition of state aid

Economic activity does not alone constitute grounds for prohibition under Art. 107(1) TFEU; other defining criteria must be met. This section of the chapter explores those criteria as they apply to an activity that has been categorised as economic. It considers how the **pricing policy** of the HEI offering the CET affects the prohibition on state aid, it looks at the further defining characteristics of "**favour**", "**market distortion**" and **"distortion of competition"**.

Preferential treatment and market-appropriate consideration through pricing

If the categorisation of the CET programme leads to the HEI's activity being classified as economic, the prohibition on state funding may not apply if no favour ensues for an undertaking.

First, a distinction must be drawn between the different levels of EU state aid rules. The favoured undertaking can either be the HEI itself or a CET institution as a third party.

Direct aid on the "first level" to the economically active HEI applies if the HEI offers its CET programmes using publicly-funded infrastructure and human resources and if the fees collected do not cover the full costs.

Indirect state aid may also apply at the "second level". For example, organisations (commercial or non-profit) that offer CET and are not part of the HEI itself can offer CET under a contract to the HEI. If the HEI made its (state-funded) infrastructure available to the CET provider and if it did not receive market-appropriate consideration for that use, then this would count as a state subsidy. If a fair market price was paid for the use of the facilities for the CET provision, then that would not count as a subsidy. This applies equally to the relationship between the HEI and its own subsidiaries, which also offer CET in co-operation with CET institutions outside the HEI sector (in Brandenburg, this is regulated in § 25(4) BbgHG.).

The chapter presents below an analysis of market-appropriate consideration, especially with regard to the case of co-operation with third parties. This is also because HEIs in Brandenburg are allowed to co-operate with non-university institutions in CET by § 25(4) BgbHG.

Market economy principle

As explained above, a state benefit for an economic activity is not an advantage if a fair market consideration is paid for it. The provision of a service at market price cannot constitute an advantage and thus cannot constitute state aid. This means that each individual case must be examined to identify if HEI infrastructure has been used in the CET programme or if HEI staff have contributed to it; and if so, whether that infrastructure or that staffing been charged out at a fair market price.

Where a fair market price does not exist, a consideration is deemed appropriate if it reflects the total cost of the service and generally includes a margin or profit or mark-up that is oriented against the mark-ups typically used by undertakings active in the same field as the service provided. Regarding the covering of costs and the inclusion of an appropriate mark-up, the ECJ required the consideration paid must cover the following three elements: i) all variable additional costs in the performance of the service; ii) an appropriate contribution to the fixed costs of the infrastructure; and iii) an appropriate return on the equity capital invested (ECJ, 2003[29]; Bartosch, 2016[18])[29].

An alternative level of consideration can be deemed appropriate only if it is the result of negotiations conducted according to the "arm's length" principle, in which the HEI negotiates as a service provider in order to extract the maximum economic benefit at the closing of the agreement, whereby it must cover at least its marginal costs. Management theory understands marginal costs as performance-specific additional costs, in other word the cost incurred by delivering one additional product (Bartosch, 2016[18])[30]. According to Point 15(f) of the R&D Framework, "arm's length" means:

> "that the conditions of the transaction between the contracting parties do not differ from those which would be stipulated between independent enterprises and contain no element of collusion. Any transaction that results from an open, transparent and non-discriminatory procedure is considered as meeting the arm's length principle." (EC, 2014[13]).

Permissibility of flat-rate charges

A flat-rate charge can also be agreed as fair market consideration.

EU state aid rules are not clear on the matter. Point 21 of the R&D Framework simply states:

> "Without prejudice to Point 20, where research organisations or research infrastructures are used to perform economic activities, such as renting out equipment or laboratories to undertakings, supplying services to undertakings or performing contract research, public funding of those economic activities will generally be considered State aid." (EC, 2014[13]).

Point 25 R&D Framework reinforces that:

> "(a) The research organisation or research infrastructure provides its research service activities or contract research activities at market price.
>
> (b) Where there is no market price, the research organisation or research infrastructure provides its **research service activity** or contract research activity at a price which:
>
> - reflects the full costs of the service and generally includes a margin established by reference to those commonly applied by undertakings active in the sector of the service concerned, or
>
> - is the result of arm's length negotiations where the research organisation or research infrastructure, in its capacity as service provider, negotiates in order to obtain the **maximum economic benefit** at the moment when the contract is concluded and covers at least its marginal costs." (EC, 2014[13]).

The wording puts "research service activity" and not "activities" as the basis for the calculation. The emphasis on the singular activity suggests that each economic activity engaged in by a HEI must be calculated according to the criteria above or the HEI would be in breach of the prohibition on state aid.

However, this approach would do justice to neither legal nor economic considerations. From a legal point of view, such an approach would be questionable because resource-intensive projects and CET programmes (such as the use of machines and laboratories) are likely to incur higher "invoice sums" in the form of contributions from participants or course fees. If the flat-rate charges for more cost-intensive CET programmes are related to the costs defrayed by the CET provider to the HEI for [other] CET programmes and are reflected in the overall costs of the HEI, then it seems possible to argue that flat-rate charges for CET programmes are compatible with EU state rules. A cost-intensive individual project can also be in conformity with the above calculation requirements, and it therefore cannot be assumed that a flat-rate charge is *per se* contrary to EU state rules[31].

EU state aid rules are legal provisions which are, of necessity, practicable and linked to economic reality. In other words, the rules create a set of boundaries within which HEIs and research institutes work but which they may not transgress. This means that the rules do not contain particular economic figures, such as the size of profit mark-ups, as economic realities can be very different depending on the Member State, the HEI or the research institute.

In addition, the EU rules on state aid follow an economic approach. They do not give primary consideration to the question of how the individual costing steps are carried out, but are concerned to see that they result in a causally just calculation of cost and that the above-mentioned framing conditions are observed. This also implies that the provisions of the R&D Framework on separate accounting can only offer general orientation. They form the framework that must be respected, but do not prescribe the concrete form.

In other words, HEIs have freedom to make choices about how they work within those boundaries, as long as they do not go outside the bounds.

Therefore, appropriate flat-rate charges, as often practised in reality, are not excluded by default if they lead to results which adhere to the legal framework. This applies particularly if they lead to a causally just allocation of costs for the use of resources between the HEI and the participants in a CET programme or any intermediary third party. Annex A contains a discussion of how HEIs might implement costing to meet the framework boundaries discussed here.

Interim conclusions

An advantage and thus the defining element of state aid can be avoided if the HEI charges a market-appropriate fee. If the fair market price is unknown, the full costs of providing services, including a reasonable profit mark-up, are to be charged. Alternatively, charges are deemed appropriate if they are the result of negotiations conducted according to the arm's-length principle in which the entity acts in its capacity as a service provider with the goal of extracting the maximum economic benefit at the conclusion of the contract, whereby it covers its marginal costs at the minimum.

When determining the market-appropriate consideration, the following points are to be given special attention when co-operating with a enterprise in the context of CET:

- **First:** A flat-rate calculation of the market-appropriate consideration does not appear to be excluded under EU state aid rules. However, such a flat rate requires continuous preliminary and final costing, i.e. a plausibility check in a periodic time frame, as well as regular evaluations and adjustment.
- **Second:** In order to be able to carry out this plausibility check where the co-operation is with a third-party undertaking, transparency between the HEI and the undertaking with which the HEI co-operates is imperative.

- **Third:** The plausibility check of the calculation presupposes that at the level of the undertaking and in accordance with the principles above, the actual use of resources of the HEI – and not merely the calculated use – are recorded and are disclosed to the HEI in a manner that allows a plausibility check, both with regard to the extent of the use of the HEI's resources and the manner in which the utilisation of resources is recorded.

Distortion of competition and impairment of inter-community trade

Market distortion and the resulting distortion of competition is a defining condition for prohibition under state aid rules. This condition relates to the existence of a potentially competitive relationship with other market participants. This also applies for a non-profit undertaking which is (or could potentially be) actively in competition with other – profit-oriented – private undertakings (EC, 1998[30]) (EC, 1998[31])[32].

The question of a potential distortion of competition was also linked to the categorisation of an activity as economic or non-economic. If the activity of the HEI, i.e. the CET programme, is in clear competition with private CET institutions, then it is possible that an activity that is actually non-economic could be classified as economic. This does not apply if no potential competitive situation can occur at all, i.e. there is no market for the programme.

However, if the potential "user" or "customer" can choose between different CET programmes for each other as equivalents with the same outcome (certifications, diplomas, admission certificates), there is a distortion of the market in favour of the subsidised CET where CET programmes offered by HEI receive public funding and are thus preferred.

As a separate criterion of Art. 107(1) TFEU, the criterion of market distortion or distortion of competition can also apply to a CET programme.

However, the existence of an advantage does not *per se* result in a market distortion (see above). It is only to be assumed if competition is likely to be influenced through the improvement of the market position of a direct beneficiary or a third party and to the detriment of another market participant, competitor, or third party (Lux-Wesener/Kamp, 2009[32])[33].

Insofar as their funding from the public purse or their use of public resources enables the HEIs to offer marketable CET programmes at a lower cost than competitors, the result could be a (potential) influence on competition. In the opinion of the ECJ, no general or clear effect on the market is required to be proven for a distortion of the market to exist; the mere potential of influence constitutes impact on trade (ECJ, 2000[33]) (Soltész, 2011[34])[34].

Therefore, it is essential to undertake an analysis and classification of many the CET programmes offered by HEIs.

The potential for *cross-border* market influence and impairment of inter-State trade must also be considered among the defining characteristics. This requirement does not apply only if the funded economic activity is a CET programme that operates or is used only locally, and which has regionally restricted impact (EC, 2012[11])[35]. The case of Prerov Logistics College, the Czech HEI that offered courses in Czech with an exclusively regional focus to its fewer than 150 students, illustrates that point. There was no expectation that students from outside the state would enrol in the course on grounds of the geographical situation, and so the EC decided that the public funding of the private school has no impact on (cross-border) trade between the Member States, even assuming that the notion of an undertaking in Art. 107(1) TFEU was fulfilled (EC, 2006[22])[36].

However, programmes which could potentially enter into cross-border competition and which do not provide the possibility of obtaining a public higher education degree could be competitive in the private CET market, so that an impairment of competition would be seen as fulfilled. The same applies if the provision of the CET programme were to be maintained without equivalent financial consideration.

Only if no supra-regional cross-border competition can – even potentially – come into existence, can a market distortion or distortion of competition (trade impairment) be ruled out, even in the case of economic activities by HEIs.

Possible justifications and exceptions to the prohibition of state aid

If a CET programme meets all the criteria of Art. 107(1) TFEU, the prohibition of state aid applies. Nevertheless, there are other possibilities for exemption from the EU ban on state aid. In detail, these are exemption under the General Block Exemption Regulation (GBER), classification as *de minimis* aid, fulfilment of the 20% clause and structuring as a service of general economic interest (SGEI). All four types are explained below.

Exemption on the basis of General Block Exemption Regulation

In certain cases, a CET programme that fulfils the criteria of Art. 107(1) TFEU may nevertheless be exempted from the prohibition of state aid under Regulation (EU) No. 651/2014 of 17 June 2014 declaring certain categories of aid compatible with the internal market in application of Articles 107 and 108 of the Treaty Text (General Block Exemption Regulation, GBER). However, the requirements are strict, meaning that there are uncertainties in the application of this exemption to CET.

First, the general conditions of the GBER are to be observed, which are detailed in Chapters I and II (Arts. 1 - 12 GBER). This means:

- **Aid must be "transparent"**, (Art. 5 GBER). The GBER focuses on whether the gross grant equivalent (essentially, the market price proxy) can be calculated without a risk assessment. According to the Regulation, certain forms of aid are generally considered transparent (Art. 5(2) GBER). If the aid is a grant, an interest rate subsidy, a guarantee, a risk finance measure or aid for the establishment of a start-up, it is considered to be "transparent" within the meaning of the GBER.
- **Aid must have an incentive effect**, (Art. 6 GBER). Aid may not to be granted for activities which a recipient would carry out under market conditions even without aid.
- In addition, **aid may not exceed the notification thresholds** of Art. 4 GBER and must be notified and published in accordance with the procedure in Arts. 9 and 11 GBER.

If an aid measure fulfils these requirements, it can be examined to see if one of the special circumstances set out in Chapter III of GBER is fulfilled.

With regard to aid for CET, the following circumstances could be of particular interest: Training aid (Art. 31 GBER); aid for compensating the costs of assistance provided to disadvantaged workers (Art. 35 GBER); aid for culture and heritage conservation (Art. 53 GBER); or aid for start-ups (Art. 22 GBER)[37]. These are described in Box 3.4.

Box 3.4. Exemption from the prohibition on state aid under the GBER

Training aid

Art. 31 GBER provides for the exemption of aid measures which concern the education and training of workers, without further defining the term "training aid". The exemption was introduced in 2014 because undertakings might be reluctant to train their employees further – to the benefit of society as a whole – for fear of losing their qualified workers (Nowak, 2016[35])[38]. This comprises all forms of aid that concern training measures but excludes aid for mandatory training (Art. 31(2) GBER) such as safety training, because in those cases, there is no need for an additional financial incentive for the training to be conducted (see Art. 6 GBER) (Nowak, 2016[35])[39]. Art. 31(4) GBER restricts the training aid to 50% of the cost; however, if the training is given:

- to disadvantaged workers, the rate is increased by 10 percentage points;
- in a medium-sized enterprise, the rate is increased by 10 percentage points;
- in a small enterprise, the rate is increased by 20 percentage points;

as long as the aid intensity is no more than 70%, overall.

Eligible costs are personnel costs for trainers (both external and in-house) (Bartosch, 2020[36])[40], costs which are incurred by the trainers (e.g. travel costs, materials), costs for advisory services and personnel costs for participants while they are taking part in the training measure.

If a HEI offers training programmes which are used by undertakings, certain elements can benefit from exemption and receive up to 50% (and no more than 70%) of costs in state aid. This takes the form of a subsidised offer from a HEI when all the relevant conditions of Chapter 1 GBER (particularly transparency, Art. 5 GBER) are met.

Disadvantaged workers

Aid granted in support of disadvantaged workers may be exempt on the basis of Art. 35 GBER. The exemption focusses on the extra costs incurred in providing support for disadvantaged workers. Aid for training staff needed to assist disadvantaged workers (Art. 35(2)(b) GBER) could be relevant for CET programmes. Such aid would be covered by the GBER, provided that the general conditions set out in Chapter I GBER are met.

Cultural heritage

Exemption on the basis of Art. 55 GBER requires the aid to be used for the conservation of cultural heritage.

This exception is particularly aimed at the maintenance of institutions such as museums, theatres and heritage sites. The exemption can also apply to training to support the maintenance of intangible heritage such as folklore, customs and crafts (Art. 53(2)(c) GBER) and activities connected with cultural and artistic education (Art. 53(2)(e) GBER. CET programmes designed to offer cultural or artistic training could therefore be exempted from the prohibition on state aid under the conditions of Chapter 1 GBER and Art. 53 *et seq* GBER.

As an example, in 2018, the EC found that funding for a bachelor's programme in music offered by a private HEI fell under the terms of Art. 53 GBER (EC, 2018[23]). However, Recital 72 of the GBER makes clear that activities may not benefit from the exemption if they have a predominantly commercial character. Therefore, an exemption on the grounds of Art. 53 GBER can be considered only on the condition that the activities are cultural or artistic education. This is unlikely to be the case for a CET programme offered by a HEI.

Aid for start-ups

An exemption from the prohibition on state aid could *prima facie* be considered if the CET programme is to be carried out by a start-up. Art. 22(3) GBER permits loans, guarantees and grants to be granted to a start-up. This applies to aid that has the form of stockholders' contributions. Grants of up to EUR 400 000 gross grant quavalent are fundamentally permissible. According to Art. 107(3)(c) TFEU, the aid may be extended to EUR 600 000 if:"the aid facilitates the development of certain economic activities or of certain economic areas, where such aid does not adversely affect trading conditions to an extent contrary to the common interest."

It is doubtful, however, that CET programmes contribute to the "development" of certain economic activities or economic areas within the meaning of Art. 107(3)(c) TFEU above. To do this, they would have to constitute an incentive to steer entrepreneurial behaviour in the direction of a specific, generally recognised economic, social or environmental objectives. As can be derived from Art. 31 GBER and Recital 53 GBER, this could be constituted by undertakings relying on CET that have positive effects for society as a whole; this is not clear, however.

If the HEI collaborates with an undertaking in the context of CET, it may also be the case that the HEI and the undertaking are deemed to be "linked undertakings" and thus no longer fall under the scope of the regulation according to Art. 22(1) GBER. It is apparent that the regulations in the BbgHG make this the case. According to Art. 3(3) Annex I, undertakings are linked if they are in one of the following relationships with another undertaking:

- an undertaking holds the majority of voting rights of the stockholders or members in another undertaking;
- an undertaking is entitled to appoint or dismiss a majority of the members of the administrative, management or supervisory body of another undertaking;
- an undertaking is entitled to exercise a controlling influence over another undertaking pursuant to an agreement entered into with that undertaking or a clause in its articles of association;
- an undertaking which is a shareholder or member of another undertaking exercises sole control over the majority of the voting rights of that undertaking's shareholders or members pursuant to an agreement entered into with other shareholders or members of that other undertaking.

According to § 25(4) BbgHG and as described, there is the possibility of co-operation with CET institutions outside the higher education sector. However, § 25(4) BbgHG limits the possibilities for HEIs to completely dispense with the task of providing CET by co-operating with institutions outside the higher education domain (Herrmann, 2018[37]). Although the organisation and delivery of the CET programme can be assigned to a co-operating institution, the HEI remains responsible for the programme content and examinations. To make legal supervision possible and executable, a co-operation agreement must be reported to the ministry responsible for higher education institutions. The HEI must therefore establish and prove a controlling influence over the co-operating institution, so that a linked enterprise can be said to exist under Art. 3(3) GBER.

Invoking an exemption under the GBER for CET with any legal certainty appears to be possible only to a narrow extent; however, such scope as exists should be exploited.

Sources: Nowak (2016[35]) in Immenga/Mestmäcker, Wettbewerbsrecht, 5. Edition; Bartosch (2020[36]), EU-Beihilfenrecht, 3. Edition; EC (2018[23]), EC decision of 08.11.2018, State aid. 43700 (2018/NN) / C(2018) 7215; Herrmann (2018[37]) in Knopp/Peine/Topel, Brandenburgisches Hochschulgesetz, 3. Auflage, § 25 Rn. 12.

Classification as de minimis aid

Invoking the provisions of the *De Minimis* Regulation does not appear to be appropriate for CET at HEIs. According to Art. 3(1) of the *De Minimis* Regulation, aid measures only fulfil the conditions of the Regulation if they do not meet all the criteria of Art. 107 TFEU. Therefore, such *de minimis* aid is exempt from the notification requirement of Art. 108(3) TFEU and no notification to the EC is required; the aid may be granted without further ado. The problem for the HEIs, however, lies in the maximum amount allowed for such aid. The total *de minimis* aid granted to a single undertaking by a Member State may not exceed EUR 200 000 over a period of three fiscal years (Art. 3(2)). This is likely to be too low a limit with regard to the funding of CET courses at HEIs.

The 20% clause

Another exception to the prohibition of state aid in Art. 107 TFEU is provided by the "20% clause" of the R&D Framework (marginal 20) for almost or near exclusive use by a research institution or research infrastructure for non-economic activities. Certain challenges remain, however, mainly because some issues have not been clarified in case law. In particular, problems may arise because control during the year appears to be particularly exacting. Another difficulty is the scope of application for this privilege in relation to CET.

The R&D Framework provides more detailed information on the scope of application of the 20% clause. According to Point 2.1.1. marginal 20 of the R&D Framework, if a research facility or research infrastructure is used almost exclusively for non-economic activities, the EC may decide that the funding falls outside state aid rules provided the economic use of the research facility or research infrastructure constitutes an **ancillary activity** that is **directly related to** and **necessary for** the operation of the research facility or research infrastructure. It seems questionable whether CET fulfils these conditions.

Alternatively, the Member State can prove that there is an inseparable link between the economic and non-economic activities[41]. Here it could be argued that, in individual cases, there is an inseparable connection between the contents of a course of study and the CET that builds on it.

In any case, the scope of the economic activity must be limited to less than 20% of the HEI's activity.

The EC made a presumption in marginal 20 of the R&D Framework:

> "For the purposes of this framework, the EC will consider this [the wording appears to refer to all the previously mentioned conditions, i.e. to the question of purely ancillary activity and of the inseparable link, and not the question of limited scope] to be the case where the economic activities consume exactly the same inputs (such as material, equipment, labour and fixed capital) as the non-economic activities and the capacity allocated each year to such economic activities does not exceed 20 % of the relevant entity's overall annual capacity." (EC, 2014[13]).

The requirements of this presumption could, in principle, be met by CET courses offered by HEIs and would then probably – the wording is not entirely clear here – be regarded as a secondary activity or activity with an inseparable link to the main activity. However, it is not possible to generalise; a precise examination of each individual case is needed.

With regard to the interpretation and application of the capacity limit of 20%, there are uncertainties in practice which have not yet been clarified either by ECJ case law or by decisions by the EC. So far, the EC has not adopted any legally binding criteria for application. In particular, it is unclear whether the reference value for capacity should be the HEI as a whole ("research institution", for definition see Point 15(ee) R&D Framework) or de-limitable units within the HEI ("research infrastructure", for definition see Point 15 (ff) R&D Framework, which also includes, for example, equipment, archives and ICT infrastructures).

The core questions of the reference figure are therefore: Can a single research institution divide itself into several sub-units, each of which constitutes research infrastructure in this sense, and must the 20% limit then apply to each of these sub-units, or should the focus be on the research institution as a single unit?

In any case, separate accounting must be conducted in order to be able to prove that the limit is not exceeded. The economic activities falling under the 20% criterion must be shown separately in the separate accounts as "privileged economic activities" (KMK, 2017[26]). With regard to the *de minimis* limit in the case of mixed use of infrastructure for non-economic and economic activities, Point 207 of the EC Notice on the notion of State aid states:

> *"If, in cases of mixed use, the infrastructure is used almost exclusively for a non-economic activity, the EC considers that its funding may fall outside the State aid rules in its entirety, provided the economic use remains purely ancillary, that is to say an activity which is directly related to and necessary for the operation of the infrastructure, or intrinsically linked to its main non-economic use. This should be considered to be the case when the economic activities consume the same inputs as the primary non-economic activities, for example material, equipment, labour or fixed capital. Ancillary economic activities must remain limited in scope, as regards the capacity of the infrastructure. Examples of such ancillary economic activities may include a research organisation occasionally renting out its equipment and laboratories to industrial partners. The EC also considers that public financing provided to customary amenities (such as restaurants, shops or paid parking) of infrastructures that are almost exclusively used for a non-economic activity normally has no effect on trade between Member States since those customary amenities are unlikely to attract customers from other Member States and their financing is unlikely to have a more than marginal effect on cross-border investment or establishment." (EC, 2016[14])*.

However, these examples are not comparable with CET, as CET programmes at HEIs are offered in competition with private HEIs and an influence on the market can therefore be expected.

Ultimately, it is uncertain how successful invoking the 20% clause would be because the EC prescribes a relatively narrow scope of application. It therefore remains uncertain whether the clause is applicable to CET programmes at all.

Consideration as SGEI

One option for making public funding of CET at HEIs compatible is to design the programmes as a service of general economic interest (SGEI). However, such an approach is subject to strict requirements, especially with regard to the clarity and transparency of the act of entrustment necessary, and this leads to a degree of legal uncertainty. There would be a risk that the act does not meet the requirements and that compensatory payments can therefore be required.

Box 3.5 below presents a justification for CET as an SGEI. A possible design will be dealt with in Chapter 5.

Box 3.5. Classification of CET as a Service of General Economic Interest (SGEI)

When is an SGEI possible?

If the aid is within the meaning of Art. 107(1) TFEU, it is subject to notification and must, in principle, comply with all substantive requirements for aid. An exception to this is provided for in Art. 106(2) TFEU for undertakings that are "entrusted" with SGEIs. The provisions of the EU Treaties, in particular the competition rules, apply to such "SGEI aid", only "in so far as the application of such rules does not obstruct the performance, in law or in fact, of the particular tasks assigned to them."

To meet the conditions for such an exemption, it is therefore clear that the SGEI in question is not provided under market conditions. Nonetheless, the financial support in question is possible under explicit primary legislation. The aim of the SGEI regulations is to ensure that the compensation provided does not distort competition. In other words, it neither compensates for a deficient company management that can be identified independently of the provision of the SGEI, nor does it overcompensate for the service actually provided.

The SGEI rules concern the special case under EU state aid rules where state aid of any kind is granted as compensation to offset the loss-making provision of SGEIs by an undertaking entrusted by the state with providing these services. The existence of an SGEI must be well justified on the basis of concrete circumstances; this creates legal risks.

In general, the entrustment of a special service task includes the provision of services which an undertaking acting in its own commercial interest would not have taken on, or would not have taken on to the same extent or under the same conditions. The EC provides an up-to-date overview of the definition of the term and how it can be used, taking into account ECJ case law, in its SGEI Communication. The SGEI Framework (EC, 2012$_{[38]}$) and the SGEI Guide (EC, 2013$_{[39]}$) prepared by the EC also provide useful information about SGEI. According to these documents, EU law does not stipulate which services are to be regarded as SGEIs and which are not. Rather, Member States and their administrations have a wide margin of discretion in determining whether a service is to be considered an SGEI (EC, 2012$_{[11]}$)[42].

> "The EC's competence in this respect is limited to checking whether the Member State has made a manifest error when defining the service as an SGEI and to assessing any State aid involved in the compensation."

According to Points 45 *et seq.* of the SGEI Communication, in this check for "manifest errors" in the SGEI definition, the EC assumes that SGEIs always have "special characteristics" compared to other economic activities. This means that services must be provided which are not in the commercial interest of the undertaking providing the service, but are in the interest of the general public and would therefore not be provided by the undertaking (or not to the same extent or under the same conditions) without the entrustment. It must be a service that the market will not provide due to lack of profitability or economic appeal. As an example, the EC cites broadband roll-out and differentiates between areas where competitive broadband services with adequate coverage are already offered (market-based service) and those where investors are not in a position to offer adequate broadband coverage (SGEI) (EC, 2012$_{[11]}$)[43].

Ultimately, the EC also considers that the services to be classified as SGEIs must be addressed to citizens or be in the interest of society as a whole (EC, 2012$_{[11]}$)[44].

Reasoning for classifying CET at HEIs as an SGEI

Arguments that the provision of CET by HEIs compensates for a market failure in the provision of an SGEI are present. However, that a service is an SGEI must be reasoned in detail in each individual case. Some examples for arguing that CET programmes can be classified as SGEI:

- The existence of an SGEI could be based on the goal of increasing the range of CET capacity of the *Land* Brandenburg. The demographic and economic changes described in Chapter 1 provide the need for Brandenburg to increase the levels of skill in its workforce. That goal is a key building block in Brandenburg's future, and also for the development of Germany's position among the EU Member States.
- Concrete arguments must be found in each individual case to make the point that funding is needed for the HEI in question to compensate for insufficient provision of CET. To achieve this, evidence is needed showing that the HEI provides supplementary CET which expands the CET capacity of the state of Brandenburg; for instance, it could be argued that CET in the medical

> field could be necessary to maintain an adequate supply of medically qualified personnel in rural areas.
>
> - Additionally, it must be argued in the specific case that providing additional CET makes a loss for the HEI. To provide concrete evidence of this, it must be shown that the provision of a given number of places on the CET course cannot be covered by tuition fees, for example because the necessary equipment for laboratories, library workspaces, microscopes, etc. cannot be funded. It must also be shown that the HEI has a financial disincentive to provide the CET.
> - It must also be shown why the provision of additional places benefits the public and serves the interest of society as a whole. As with the expansion of broadband internet, CET can use the argument that the state of Brandenburg cannot provide the appropriate education and training capacity for itself in any other way. The cost of setting up or expanding a programme could exceed the financial means of the HEI so that an entrustment act is necessary.
> - A further justification could be that only if the number of places for CET courses, for example in the field of medicine, is increased can adequate health care be safeguarded.
> - It is also of interest to know whether models exist for binding graduates professionally to Brandenburg, such as scholarships, for example. Data on how many graduates stay in Brandenburg after completing their CET programme are relevant in this respect too. If graduates tend to leave the state and there are no programmes binding them to the state, the act of entrustment should show how the HEI tries to bind the students in the CET programme to the state of Brandenburg as part of its curriculum. For example, the programme can create a clear link to state and can establish a justified expectation that graduates will stay in the state upon completion.
>
> Sources: EC (2012[11]), Communication from the Commission — European Union framework for State aid in the form of public service compensation (2011) Text with EEA relevance; EC (2013[39]), Guide to the application of the European Union rules on state aid, public procurement and the internal market to services of general economic interest, and in particular to social services of general economic interest, of 29.04.2013, SWD(2013) 53 final/2; EC (2012[38]), Communication from the Commission on the application of the European Union State aid rules to compensation granted for the provision of services of general economic interest.

Interim conclusion on classifying CET in terms of EU state aid rules

The presentation of the classification of CET under EU law in Art. 107(1) TFEU is intended to identify when CET can be considered free of the prohibition of state aid. The question is therefore under which conditions EU state aid rules do not apply to CET offered by HEIs. If EU state aid rules are at least partially applicable to CET at HEIs, the question arises as to the adjustment measures HEIs need to consider.

Classification of CET at public HEIs in terms of EU state aid rules

It was highlighted above that there are no clear guidelines from the EC or the ECJ for classifying CET at HEIs as an economic activity or non-economic activity. In particular, the EC does not explicitly classify CET as a generally non-economic activity. This is why the demarcation criteria summarised above are important. According to these criteria, CET can be problematic from a legal point of view, in particular if it has to compete with the private sector and is not predominantly financed through public funds.

Consequences of classifying CET at HEIs as an economic activity

Insofar as EU state aid criteria suggest that a certain CET offering constitutes an economic activity, the other constituent elements of Art. 107(1) TFEU must be assessed first. Only then can possible justifications for the aid and exceptions to the prohibition of aid be considered.

The first aspect to review is whether the HEI as an undertaking (or an undertaking co-operating with the HEI) is a favoured party. If fees paid by the participants or the third-party institution are in line with market prices, treatment as a favoured party may no longer apply, and the prohibition of state aid then also does not apply. How market-appropriate remuneration is to be structured must be determined for each CET programme on a case-by-case basis.

Secondly, the existing or potential market situation must be examined to see whether cross-border trade in services between the Member States could be affected by the CET programme in question. The requirement for this is that the programme may cause a distortion of competition.

Only when these defining conditions are met does the prohibition of state aid apply. The CET programme can still be justified, however, or can be subject to an exception.

With regard to possible exceptions to the prohibition of state aid, the first option is to classify HEI funding as an SGEI. It seems less promising and recommendable to attempt to exempt the aid under the GBER, classify it as *de minimis* aid and resort the 20% clause.

References

Bartosch (ed.) (2020), *EU-Beihilfenrecht, 3. Auflage*.	[36]
Bartosch (ed.) (2016), *EU-Beihilfenrecht, 2. Auflage*.	[18]
Callies/Ruffert (ed.) (2016), *TEU/TFEU, 5. Auflage 2016*.	[9]
EC (2018), *EC decision of 08.11.2018, State aid. 43700 (2018/NN) / C(2018) 7215*, https://ec.europa.eu/competition/state_aid/cases/276053/276053_2028505_63_2.pdf.	[23]
EC (2016), *Commission Notice on the notion of State aid as referred to in Article 107(1) of the Treaty on the Functioning of the European Union, OJ C 262 of 19.07.2016*.	[14]
EC (2014), *Communication from the Commission on Framework for State aid for research and development and innovation*.	[13]
EC (2013), *Guide to the application of the European Union rules on state aid, public procurement and the internal market to services of general economic interest, and in particular to social services of general interest, of 29.04.2013, SWD(2013) 53 final/2*.	[39]
EC (2012), *Communication from the Commission — European Union framework for State aid in the form of public service compensation (2011) Text with EEA relevance*.	[38]
EC (2012), *Communication from the Commission on the application of the European Union State aid rules to compensation granted for the provision of services of general economic interest*.	[11]
EC (2009), *Common principles for an economic assessment of the compatibility of state aid under Art. 87.3*.	[17]
EC (2009), *Common Principles for an Economic Assessment of the Compatibility of State Aid under Article 87(3) of the EC Treaty*, http://ec.europa.eu/competition/state_aid/reform/economic_assessment_en.pdf.	[16]
EC (2008), *EC decision of 26.11.2008, State aid No N 343/2008*, https://ec.europa.eu/competition/state_aid/cases/226491/226491_917103_29_1.pdf.	[24]
EC (2006), *EC Decision of 08.11.2006, State aid No N 54/2006*, https://ec.europa.eu/competition/state_aid/cases/216285/216285_609589_14_1.pdf.	[22]
EC (2005), *State aid action plan - Less and better targeted state aid : a roadmap for state aid reform 2005-2009 (Consultation document) {SEC(2005) 795}, COM/2005/0107 final*.	[15]
EC (2003), *EC Decision of 01.10.2003, State aid No N 37/2003*, https://ec.europa.eu/competition/state_aid/cases/133835/133835_469556_45_2.pdf.	[25]
EC (1998), *Commission notice on the application of the State aid rules to measures relating to direct business taxation, OJ EC C 384 of 10.12.1998*.	[31]
EC (1998), *Commissioner Decision 98/353/EC of 16.09.1997 on State aid for Gemeinnützige Abfallverwertung GmbH, OJ EC L 159 of 03.06.1998*.	[30]
EC (1997), *Commission Notice on the definition of relevant market for the purposes of Community competition law, OJ C 372, 9.12.1997*.	[28]

ECJ (2019), *Judgment of 04.07.2019 – C-393/17*, GRUR. [8]

ECJ (2010), *Judgment of 20.05.2010 – C-56/09*, IStR. [7]

ECJ (2007), *Judgment of 11.09.2007 – C-76/95*, NJW. [6]

ECJ (2006), *Judgment of 10.01.2006 – C-222/04*, EuZW. [3]

ECJ (2006), *Judgment of 23.03.2006 – C-237/04*, BeckRS. [10]

ECJ (2005), *Judgment of 03.03.2005 – C-172/03*, BeckRS. [20]

ECJ (2001), *Judgment of 08.11.2001 – C-143/99*, NVwZ. [19]

ECJ (2000), *Judgment of 19.09.2000 – C-156/98*, EuZW. [33]

ECJ (1993), *Judgment of 07.12.1993 – C-109/92*, BeckRS. [5]

ECJ (1991), *Judgment of 23.04.1991 – C-41/90*, NJW. [1]

ECJ (1988), *Judgment of 27.09.1988 – C-263/86*, BeckRS. [4]

EFTA Court (2008), *Judgment of 21.02.2008 – E-5/07*, https://eftacourt.int/download/5-07-judgment/?wpdmdl=1631. [12]

EuZW (ed.) (2003), *Judgment of 03.07.2003 – joined cases C-83/01 P, C-93/01 P and C-94/01*. [29]

Hartmer/Detmer (ed.) (2009), *Hochschulrecht [Higher education law], 2. Auflage*. [32]

Immenga/Mestmäcker (ed.) (2016), *Wettbewerbsrecht, 5. Auflage*. [35]

Immenga/Mestmäcker (ed.) (2016), *Wettbewerbsrecht, Band 3, 5. Auflage 2016*. [2]

KMK (2017), *Leitfaden zur Unterscheidung wirtschaftlicher und nichtwirtschaftlicher Tätigkeit von Hochschulen [Guide to Distinguishing Economic and Non-economic Activity of Universities]*, https://www.kmk.org/fileadmin/Dateien/veroeffentlichungen_beschluesse/2017/2017_09_22-Leitfaden-Wirtschaftliche-Nichtwirtschaftliche-Taetigkeit.pdf. [26]

Knopp/Peine/Topel (ed.) (2018), *Brandenburgisches Hochschulgesetz [Brandenburg Higher Education Act], 3. Auflage, § 25 Rn. 12*. [37]

Marwedel (2014), *Rechtsgutachten zu Vorgaben für die Preisgestaltung der wissenschaftlichen Weiterbildung an der Universität Freiburg unter besonderer Berücksichtigung des europäischen Beihilferechts*, [Legal opinion on specifications for the pricing of scientific further education at the University of Freiburg with special consideration of European state aid law]. [27]

Mederer, V. (2015), *AEUV, 7. Auflage*. [21]

Montag/Säcker (ed.) (2011), *MüKo zum Europäischen und Deutschen Wettbewerbsrecht, Band 3, 1. Auflage*. [34]

Notes

[1] According to ECJ case law, first in Judgment of 23.04.1991 – C-41/90, NJW 1991, 2891, 2891 f., marginal 21.

[2] Mestmäcker/Schweitzer in: Immenga/Mestmäcker, Wettbewerbsrecht, Band 3, 5. Auflage 2016, Art. 107 AEUV marginal 17.

[3] ECJ, Judgment of 10.01.2006 – C-222/04, EuZW 2006, 306, 311 f., marginal 122.

[4] ECJ, Judgment of 10.01.2006 – C-222/04, EuZW 2006, 306, 311 f., marginal 123.

[5] See ECJ, Judgment of 27.09.1988 – C-263/86, BeckRS 2004, 72754, marginal 17.

[6] ECJ, Judgment of 27.09.1988 – C-263/86, BeckRS 2004, 72754.

[7] ECJ, Judgment of 07.12.1993 – C-109/92, BeckRS 2004, 74113, marginal 15 ff.

[8] ECJ, Judgment of 11.09.2007 – C-76/95, NJW 2008, 351, 353.

[9] ECJ, Judgment of 20.05.2010 – C-56/09, IStR 2010, 487, 488.

[10] ECJ, Judgment of 04.07.2019 – C-393/17, GRUR 2019, 846.

[11] Opinion of Advocate General at ECJ, 15.11.2018 – C-393/17, BeckRS 2018, 28556, marginal 52 ff.; on the issues raised by the Advocate General, see Hillemann/Wittig, OdW 2019, 169.

[12] Opinion of Advocate General at ECJ, 15.11.2018 – C-393/17, BeckRS 2018, 28556, marginal 73.

[13] Cremer in: Calliess/Ruffert, EUV/AEUV, 5. Auflage 2016, Art. 107 AEUV marginal 27.

[14] ECJ, Judgment of 23.03.2006 – C-237/04, BeckRS 2006, 70228, marginal 28 with further references to established ECJ case law.

[15] Communication from the Commission on the application of the European Union State aid rules to compensation granted for the provision of services of general economic interest, OJ C 8 of 11.01.2012, p. 4

[16] EFTA Court, Judgment of 21.02.2008 – E-5/07, marginal 80 f, available at: https://eftacourt.int/download/5-07-judgment/?wpdmdl=1631.

[17] For the tasks of the EC in EU state aid law, see Art. 108 TFEU.

[18] SGEI Communication (footnote 101), marginal 26.

[19] SGEI Communication (footnote 101), marginal 28.

[20] Communication from the Commission on Framework for State aid for research and development and innovation, 198/01, marginal 19(a), 2014/C 198/01.

[21] Commission Notice on the notion of State aid (marginal 28).

[22] Commission Notice on the notion of State aid (marginal 28).

[23] The "strong economically oriented approach" is to be used only in the examination of the compatibility of state aid with the internal market, in particular of its proportionality and impact on competition. The approach is not intended for the examination of whether state aid is present at all. EC's discretionary power in deciding whether state aid is present is limited to carrying out complex economic evaluations.

[24] Bartosch, EU-Beihilferecht, 2. Auflage 2016, marginal 5.

[25] ECJ, Judgment of 08.11.2001 – C-143/99, NVwZ 2002, 842, 844, marginal 41; ECJ, judgment of 03.03.2005 – C-172/03, BeckRS 2005, 70158, marginal 40.

[26] Von der Groeben/Schwarze/Wolfgang Mederer, AEUV, 7. Auflage 2015, Art. 107 marginal 12.

[27] It says: "…DETERMINED to promote the development of the highest possible level of knowledge for their peoples through a wide access to education and through its continuous updating …"

[28] ECJ, Judgment of 10.01.2006 – C-222/04, EuZW 2006, 306, 311f., marginal 123.

[29] ECJ, Judgment of 03.07.2003 – joined cases C-83/01 P, C-93/01 P and C-94/01 P, EuZW 2003, 504, 509, Rn. 40.

[30] Bartosch/Bartosch, EU-Beihilfenrecht, 2. Auflage 2016, AEUV Art. 107 Rn. 128.

[31] Flat-rate charges can be charged for repetitive services such as courses where the market price or cost structure including profit margin is fixed and can be determined transparently. Ideally, the flat-rate charges should be reviewed and updated.

[32] Commissioner Decision 98/353/EC of 16.09.1997 on State aid for Gemeinnützige Abfallverwertung GmbH, OJ EC L 159 of 03.06.1998, p. 58; see also Commission notice on the application of the State aid rules to measures relating to direct business taxation, OJ EC C 384 of 10.12.1998, p. 3, marginal 25: "non-profit-making undertakings, such as foundations or associations".

[33] Lux-Wesener/Kamp, in: Hartmer/Detmer, Hochschulrecht, 2. Auflage 2009, Kapitel VIII, marginal 47.

[34] See ECJ, Judgment of 19.09.2000 – C-156/98, EuZW 2000, 723, 725, marginal 39; also Soltész, in: Montag/Säcker, MüKo zum Europäischen und Deutschen Wettbewerbsrecht, Band 3, 1. Auflage 2011, Art. 107 AEUV, marginal 414.

[35] See EC (2012), Communication from the Commission on the application of the European Union State aid rules to compensation granted for the provision of services of general economic interest, p. 10.

[36] The presence of just a marginal "cross-border" effect would already be enough to rule out impact on intra-Community trade.

[37] In addition, aid for innovation cluster operators could also be considered, in particular "the organisation of training measures" according to Art. 28 (8)c, GBER. However, since such aid is likely to be rare in practice, it will not be discussed in more detail.

[38] Nowak in: Immenga/Mestmäcker, Wettbewerbsrecht, 5. Auflage 2016, Art. 31 AGVO Rn. 1.

[39] Nowak in: Immenga/Mestmäcker, Wettbewerbsrecht, 5. Auflage 2016, Art. 31 AGVO Rn. 6.

[40] Bartosch in: Bartosch, EU-Beihilfenrecht, 3. Auflage 2020, Art. 31 AGVO Rn. 3.

[41] See ECJ, Judgment of 26.3.2009 – C-113/07 P, BeckRS 2009, 70333, marginal 118 f.; Judgment of 12.7.2012 – C-138/11 EuZW 2012, 835, 836, marginal 38. On the practice of the Commission: EU Commission decision of 19.7.2006, N 140/2006, OJ 2006 C 244, p. 12: In the case of aid to public undertakings which provide vocational training and employment for prisoners in correctional facilities, the objective of promoting employment and reintegration cannot be separated from the sovereign activity of the prison system; decision of 27.6.2007, N 558/2005, OJ 2007 C 255, p. 22: When employing severely disabled people with a view to their independence and reintegration, the products and services they produce are merely an ancillary economic activity.

[42] See Points 45-46 of the SGEI Communication; see also ECJ, Judgment of 12.12.1973 – 127/73, GRUR Int. 1974, 342, 345; CJEU, Judgment of 15.06.2005 – T-17/02, BeckRS 2005, 70448, marginal 216; CJEU, Judgment of 26.06.2008 – T-442/03, ZUM 2008, 766, 769, marginal 195.

[43] SGEI Communication (footnote 101), Point 49.

[44] SGEI Communication (footnote 101), Point 50.

4 CET in practice at HEIs in Brandenburg

This chapter looks at the actual practices of Brandenburg's HEIs in their implementation of CET programmes. It draws from information provided by seven Brandenburg HEIs about the types of CET programmes they offer – including academic programmes, certificate courses, vocational development courses and language courses, among others. The HEIs also reported on how they organise, implement and manage CET programmes. These approaches are then assessed against the legal principles established in Chapters 2 and 3. This chapter also offers comparative analysis of the CET practices of Brandenburg's HEIs with those of HEIs in Bavaria, Hesse and North Rhine-Westphalia.

The situation at Brandenburg's HEIs

Chapter 3 outlined the criteria used in determining whether (and if so, how) the EU state aid rules apply to CET in HEIs. This chapter now turns to the extent to which the actual CET programmes offered by Brandenburg's HEIs comply with the criteria for non-economic activities.

The State of Brandenburg is home to eight public higher education institutions (HEIs) – four universities (Brandenburg University of Technology Cottbus-Senftenberg, European University Viadrina Frankfurt/Oder, Film University Babelsberg Konrad Wolf, and University of Potsdam) and four universities of applied sciences (Brandenburg University of Applied Sciences, University for Sustainable Development Eberswalde, University of Applied Sciences Potsdam, and Technical University of Applied Sciences Wildau) – and two specialised HEIs in public administration (*Verwaltungsfachhochschulen*). Beside these, there are two HEIs funded by churches and three private institutions.

The basis for the discussion in this chapter is information supplied by seven of the eight public HEIs in Brandenburg[1] via responses to a questionnaire, which was developed for the purpose of giving the legal analysis an empirical basis.

Evaluation of the questionnaire

The questionnaire aimed initially to explore the basic approach and the fundamental methods of dealing with CET of any kind at the HEIs. In addition, it was intended to provide an overview of the CET offerings of Brandenburg's HEIs and the environment in which these offerings operate.

Accordingly, the questionnaire is divided into two sections. In the first section, the questions aim to ascertain the level of knowledge at the participating HEIs with regard to classifying courses and programmes in terms of their relevance to EU state aid rules. In the second section, the questions aim to discover more about the different CET offerings of Brandenburg's higher education institutions. The corresponding categories of CET offerings are set out below as clusters. These are CET programmes, such as:

- CET degree-awarding programmes such as MBA degrees;
- study programme modules and certificate courses;
- vocational development courses/events (*berufliche Fortbildungsveranstaltungen*);
- extracurricular language courses;
- CET offerings such as lectures, courses, workshops that are open to both students and third parties;
- co-operative study programmes.

Knowledge of relevant terms for classifying an activity under EU state aid rules

The answers to the first set of questions show that the great majority of the participating HEIs work with the framework for classifying an activity under EU state aid rules and are familiar with the essential distinctions.

The legal framework is generally known to the participating HEIs, but fewer than half of the respondents knew the SGEI Communication or the concept of aid compatible with the common market (*vereinbare Beihilfe*). An assessment tool to distinguish between economic and non-economic activities exists at almost every HEI surveyed. Five of the seven HEIs organise CET either through a special-purpose enterprise or an enterprise of a commercial nature.

CET degree-awarding programmes (Weiterbildungsstudiengänge) cluster

The first cluster concerns degree-awarding programmes, for example, MBA degrees. Six of the seven participating HEIs offer such a degree. Most of these programmes are offered for a fee. Two-thirds of the programmes offered are costed using the full-cost method (see Annex A for a discussion of costing approaches) and one-third are priced using the partial cost method. Of those that calculate on a partial cost basis, all indicated that the fee component is a maximum of 50% of the full cost. Only one of the six HEIs does not see itself in competition with private providers; three other HEIs stated that their programmes are partially in competition with private providers. Three responses indicate that private providers do not offer these programmes due to a lack of the necessary expertise and/or resources, while three others stated that they were unaware of why private providers did not offer these programmes, and one expressed the view that only public HEIs can offer such programmes.

Certificate courses cluster

This cluster includes study programme modules and certificate courses which are not incorporated into a complete study programme. All seven HEIs offer these kinds of courses, and six of the seven fund them exclusively by charging fees, whereby the calculation is done using the full-cost method. All of the HEIs consider themselves to be in competition (two of them at least partially) with private providers.

Vocational development courses/events (berufliche Fortbildungsveranstaltungen) cluster

Vocational development courses/events do not require participants to have a higher education degree, but can be completed with or without a certificate. All respondents also indicated that their HEI offers courses of this kind, six of them fully funded by fees and the other one partially fee-funded. The fees were calculated using the full-cost method by six of the seven HEIs. All of the HEIs consider themselves to be in competition (two of them at least partially) with private providers. The three responses to the question about the reasons for the lack of private providers indicated that private providers did not offer such courses because they lack the necessary expertise and/or resources.

Language courses cluster

CET programmes include language courses outside of the regular curriculum of study programmes. Five of the seven higher education institutions indicated that they offer such extracurricular language courses, two of them as partially fee-funded and two as as fully fee-funded. The basis for calculation was given by three HEIs, with an inconclusive result. But here, too, the five HEIs are fully or partially in competition with private providers.

Lectures, courses, workshops and other offerings cluster

Five out of seven HEIs indicate that they offer CET in the form of lectures, courses, workshops and other offerings that are accessible to both students and third parties. Here, a diverse picture emerges with regard to whether fees are charged (Yes = one HEI; No = two HEIs; Partial = two HEIs). Of the three HEIs that charge fees, two stated that the fee is calculated using the full-cost method and the other HEI stated that it is calculated using the partial cost method. The majority of HEIs see themselves at least partly in competition with private providers in this cluster as well. With regard to the lack of private offerings, two respondents stated that private providers did not offer services in the field due to a lack of expertise or resources.

Co-operative study programmes cluster

The final block of questions aimed to gather information about co-operative study programmes on offer. Only one responding HEI indicated that it offered a study programme in co-operation with another organisation. It is offered on an exclusively fee-charging basis, whereby the fee is calculated using the full-cost method. The programme stands in competition with offerings from private providers.

Assessment of the clusters with regard to the delimiting criteria in EU state aid rules

The following section assesses how the various CET offerings in higher education can be classified using the EU state aid rules criteria. In the process, the particular legal difficulties that exist in the differentiation between economic and non-economic activities will be discussed.

Assessment of the CET degree-awarding programmes cluster

CET degree-awarding programmes are offered by almost all participating Brandenburg HEIs.

With regard to *competition from private organisations*, it is significant that half of the responding HEIs perceive themselves to be at least partially in competition with private providers. This implies that they are engaged in an economic activity.

With regard to the *financing structure*, two-thirds of the CET study programmes are offered for a fee on a full-cost basis. This means that private funding is involved, which speaks in favour of a commercial activity. The other third of the study programmes are at least 50% funded by the state (meaning that they are predominantly publicly funded). What matters here is how the private competition criterion relates to the public funding criterion, in any case insofar as the study programmes in question can be said to be competing.

No HEI reports an *intention to make a profit*.

Regarding *integration into the state education system*, CET study programmes at German public HEIs are deeply integrated into the state education system. This is, above all, the result of how higher education is organised and the official oversight of higher education institutions.

Turning to the potential *public interest in CET study programmes*, at least one HEI does not see itself as being in competition with private organisations at all. This is the case because the public HEIs are of the opinion that private providers cannot offer CET programmes, as they lack the necessary expertise and/or resources, or that only public HEIs can offer CET programmes of this type. In those areas where the private sector is not effective, a special public interest could be deemed to exist in order that CET can be offered at all.

The private competition and the predominantly private funding mentioned above all speak in favour of classifying these CET programmes as economic activities undertaken by the HEIs under the currently applicable criteria of EU state aid rules.

Assessment of the certificate courses cluster

Certificate courses that are not part of a full study programme are offered by all participating HEIs. The criterion of private funding through fees on a full-cost basis is particularly salient here. The higher education institutions also face – at least partially – *private competition*.

However, an *intention to make a profit* cannot be established in this cluster either.

Integration into the state education system is unequivocal, as the courses are offered by public HEIs.

However, the clearly perceptible competition with private providers means that the *special public interest* must be seen as being lower here than for CET study programmes.

Among these CET programmes, the thresholds for classification as non-economic are regularly breached, implying that this is *prima facie* economic activity. The result would be different only if *integration into the state education system* were to be regarded as a sufficient condition of non-economic activity. However, more compelling reasons speak against this due to the objective of EU state aid rules (on the problem of the order of priority of delimiting criteria).

Assessment of the advanced training courses cluster

All responding HEIs also offer advanced training courses.

The competition criterion is also clear in this cluster, as the HEIs consider themselves to be *competing mostly with private providers*.

The large majority of the offerings are fee-based, with the fees calculated using the full-cost method, meaning that the criterion of *predominantly private funding* is also met.

Integration into the state education system could be used to argue that the activity is non-economic, depending on how heavily this criterion is weighted. This cannot be established with any degree of certainty, however.

It is more difficult to discern a *special public or state interest*, as the presence of apparently vibrant competition from private providers means that the state has relatively little interest in filling an apparent gap in CET provision.

Assessment of language courses cluster

The majority of responding HEIs also have offerings in the language courses cluster.

All these offerings are – at least partially – in *competition with those of private providers*.

Looking at *source of funding*, the language courses are generally offered for a fee, but there are courses that are offered free of charge and that are thus substantially state-funded. One HEI indicated that it calculated fee charge using the partial cost method, covering 50% of the costs. If state funding is more than 50% in this case, the courses would also be deemed as substantially state-funded.

As language courses offered by institutes in the state education system, they are clearly *integrated into the state education system*.

There may be a *special state interest* in certain language courses, in accordance with the KMK guidelines (for example, events of the German Academic Exchange Service, *Deutscher Akademischer Austauschdienst*, DAAD). Otherwise, however, the presence of robust private competition speaks more in favour of the classification of language courses as economic activities.

Assessment of the lectures, courses, workshops and other offerings cluster

CET in this cluster is offered by the overwhelming majority of responding HEIs.

The majority of the offerings are seen to have *competition from the private sector*, but not all. This appears to indicate that some of the activities in this cluster are to be seen as non-economic.

Looking at source of funding, there are a number of activities offered free of charge, meaning that they are state-funded. This could, therefore, also be a field that could be classified as non-economic.

Integration into the state education system is also established.

The *special public interest* could arise, in particular, from the fact that private competition in this cluster is perceived to be relatively weak. There seems to be a particularly clear "supply gap" here, which the state must close with its own resources in order to fulfil its CET mandate.

Assessment of the co-operative study programmes cluster

Co-operative study programmes are predominantly *privately funded* and face the presence of *competition from private providers*.

Summary assessment of the **competition from private providers** criterion

In terms of EU state aid rules, the competition situation is problematic when private providers are present. This is particularly relevant in the case of co-operation in CET provision with another enterprise/ undertaking.

It can be deduced from the responses of the HEIs that certain "competition-free" areas exist. However, the vast majority of situations in all of the clusters must be presumed to involve competition, and this makes competition a general obstacle to classifying the CET provision here as non-economic. However, the EC has yet to clarify if that constitutes grounds for CET to be classified as economic.

Summary assessment of **state funding** and **profit intention**

CET practice at HEIs in Brandenburg shows that CET is offered in several categories for a fee that covers the full costs and cannot therefore be said to be "substantially" funded by the state. The fact that several categories of CET provided is not fully publicly funded or predominantly publicly funded speaks against them being classified as non-economic.

It can make a difference from the point of view of EU state aid rules whether the HEI intends to make a profit with a specific CET offering by charging fees, or whether it merely intends to cover its costs. After evaluating the questionnaire, it appears that where the HEIs charge fees, they do so on the basis of covering all their costs at the most, meaning that the categories of CET offered by the HEIs in question here are not offered with the intention of making a profit. This can be used to argue in favour of classification as non-economic activities. Case law and EC practice is not clear on this matter, however, and so the lack of intention to profit cannot be said with certainty to be a sufficient condition to constitute a non-economic activity.

Summary assessment of **integration into the state education system**

The EC's decision on the private Czech HEI, Prerov Logistics College, emphasised the integration of the private institution into the state education system for qualification as a non-economic activity. Brandenburg's public HEIs are bound to the state's Higher Education Act (BbgHG), meaning that they have control and responsibility for the oversight of their CET offerings but that they are under the authority of the state within the framework of higher education organisation. As a result, it can be argued on very good grounds that the criteria of state oversight is fulfilled with regard to the activities in question.

With regard to the EC's decision practice, this could be decisive in classifying the activities as non-economic.

Overall assessment **of special public interest in CET at HEIs**

With regard to a special public interest in CET by public HEIs, this study shows that there is a certain lack of offers from private providers – at least in the opinion of the responding HEIs. The HEIs are of the opinion that private providers lack expertise and resources in this area. For example, the answers to questions about CET academic programmes indicate that private offerings are not offered due to lack of the necessary expertise and/or lack of the necessary resources, or that they are unknown to the HEIs, or that only public HEIs can provide such offerings.

It is precisely where such "gaps in supply" of CET in science can be identified that a particular public interest in provision by the state could arise. The need for CET provision is recognised both politically and legally in Germany. And where private institutions cannot – for whatever reason – be sufficiently active, the only option is to provide CET through public HEIs.

However, it should be noted that this criterion has not yet been sufficiently elaborated by case law and the EC. Although the KMK Guidelines mention it clearly, the Guidelines are not legally binding, and therefore clarification by the EC in this regard is desirable. Accordingly, relying solely on special public interest as a criterion is currently fraught with legal uncertainties, in the case of privately funded offerings.

Overall assessment of other constituting elements of the prohibition of state aid

Since the public funding of the HEIs is not open to question, the assessment of the CET practice at Brandenburg's HEIs still depends on the constituting elements of preferential treatment and the distortion of competition and the resulting effect on intra-community trade.

With regard to preferential treatment, it is noticeable that the fees are mostly calculated on a full-cost basis, and this can prevent the fulfilment of the constituting element as state aid, since CET can then be designed in a budget-neutral way. However, a proper separate accounting is still necessary. Particular attention must also be paid that fees are market-appropriate. In principle, flat-rate charges can also be part of a permissible pricing strategy.

As regards the distortion of competition and the effect on intra-community trade, competition exists with private suppliers in most areas, but it is necessary to determine in each case not only whether a market exists at all for the CET offering, but also whether that CET is restricted to a local area. Because EU state aid rules only apply to economic activities that are relevant to the single market, if there are sufficient local restrictions on the continuing education offering, the constituting element of state aid would not be fulfilled.

Overall assessment of possible justifications and exceptions to the prohibition of state aid

It is not possible to deduce from the survey of the HEIs whether the possibilities for justifying and exempting CET from the prohibition of state aid were exploited and, if so, how. It is, however, striking that four our of the seven responding HEIs stated that they were not aware of the SGEI Communication. It can therefore be assumed that not all HEIs are aware of the significant possibilities for structuring higher education funding.

Classification of CET offered in other *Länder*

To put the practice at higher education institutes in Brandenburg in relation to that in other relevant states, the following discussion uses information available in the public domain to present information on CET programmes offered by public HEIs in Bavaria, Hesse and North Rhine-Westphalia.

CET offered by public HEIs in Bavaria

CET is also anchored in the state education system in Bavaria. According to publicly available information, however, the offerings are generally not fully funded by the state.

CET at Bavarian HEIs is embedded in both the Bavarian Constitution and the Bavarian Higher Education Act (BayHSchG). Art. 139 of the Bavarian Constitution regulates the funding of adult education by adult education centres and other publicly-funded institutions. According to Art. 2(1) BayHSchG, HEIs in Bavaria serve to nurture and develop the sciences and the arts by means of research, teaching, study and **continuing education and training** in a free, democratic and social state governed by the rule of law.

Art. 2(5) BayHSchG defines academic continuing education as part of the mandate of HEIs. Study programmes may also be offered as **part-time study programmes** in accordance with Art. 56(4) BayHSchG. In addition, modular courses of study for the acquisition of academic or professional partial qualifications may be offered pursuant to Art. 56(6) BayHSchG, in which individual modules of an undergraduate or postgraduate course of study are completed. Supplementary study courses in which further partial qualifications are acquired in parallel to an undergraduate or postgraduate study course, as well as special further education studies, may also be offered.

The legal requirements provide for a mixed public-private funding structure, in which funding for individual offerings may be primarily or exclusively public or private. For part-time degree programmes, HEIs charge fees in relation to the increased expenditure incurred by offering the degree programme (see Art. 56(4) and Art. 71(2) BayHSchG). Accordingly, the HEI or the faculty in question must prepare a cost or fee calculation for the planned degree programme (Baudach; Fraunhofer; Heese et al., 2014[1]). In accordance with § 2(2) to (4) of the Higher Education Fee Ordinance (HschGebV), the fee is based on the scope of the courses. However, a fee framework is set and, pursuant to to § 2(3) HschGebV, the maximum fee is EUR 200 per person per [class] hour. For part-time studies, § 2(4) HschGebV provides for fees up to a maximum of EUR 2000 per semester. Accordingly, it can be assumed that the fees do not cover all costs in every case. It is therefore possible that individual offerings are substantially state-funded.

CET offered by public HEIs in Hesse

The findings are similar in Hesse. CET is clearly integrated into the public education system. However, the costs of the individual offerings are generally to be covered by fees. This means that there is generally a lack of substantially publicly-funded offerings.

CET at HEIs in Hesse is regulated in § 16 of the Higher Education Act of Hesse (HessHG), supplemented by § 7(1) of the Hessian Continuing Education and Training Act (HWBG). § 16 HessHG stipulates that HEIs should develop and offer CET programmes to deepen academic knowledge and supplement practical vocational experience. Co-operation with private institutions is also provided for in § 3(9) HessHG to expand CET programmes. The various CET programmes, such as master's degree programmes, CET programmes with certificates and postgraduate study programmes, are structured differently by the HEIs.

Pursuant to § 16(3) HessHG, fees must be charged which cover the costs "in total". The governing body (*Präsidium*) of the HEI is responsible for setting the fees.

CET offered by public HEIs in North Rhine-Westphalia

North Rhine-Westphalia is the most populous *Land* in Germany, and there are correspondingly more HEIs than in Brandenburg, with 14 universities, 16 universities of applied sciences and seven public colleges of art and music. The legal survey shows that CET is also legally anchored here in the state education system as a mandate of higher education. However, programmes are to cover their costs through fees and charges. This speaks clearly in favour of them being classified as substantially privately funded.

§ 62 of the Higher Education Act of North Rhine-Westphalia (HG NRW) regulates scientific and artistic CET at HEIs in a similar way to the BbgHG. However, the options for HEIs in the area of CET differ. According to § 25(4) BbgHG, co-operation with "suitable institutions" outside the higher education sector may be entered into in order to provide CET, as long as the higher education institution remains responsible for the content and examinations. § 62(2) HG NRW opens up the possibility, in principle, of offering CET in a form governed by public law or by private law. Co-operation with (private) third parties is possible for the purpose of offering CET, § 3(3) HG NRW. Special provision is also made for the possibility of offering language courses that are a prerequisite for admission to higher education, as well as preparatory courses that can be offered on a private-law basis pursuant to the fourth sentence of § 48(10) HG NRW.

Pursuant to § 62 (5) sentence 1 HG NRW, a cost-covering charge should be set for CET programmes offered under public law, while fees should be levied for CET programmes offered under private law.[2] The statutory instruction to finance public-law CET so as to cover its costs speaks in favour of classifying the corresponding activities as economic activities.

Interim summary of the situation in Bavaria, Hesse and North Rhine-Westphalia

The structuring of the role and the requirements for CET offered by HEIs in the different *Länder* sheds light on the key role that the state legislatures assign to HEIs in the field of CET.

Specific features of the *Länder* must also be taken into account; for example, the question of which instruments under private law HEIs can avail themselves of in the area of CET. Particularly relevant in this respect is that the evidence shows that CET activities of HEIs are clearly integrated into the state education system, yet it cannot be assumed that CET provision is substantially funded by the state.

This means that the problem of the order of priority of the delimitation criteria reappears. This is particularly the case since, in view of the many private CET providers in Germany, private competition with state providers can be taken as a given. Against the backdrop of this funding structure, it cannot be assumed with any legal certainty that the EC would regard the offerings in question as non-economic.

References

Baudach; Fraunhofer; Heese et al. (2014), *Leitfaden zur Entwicklung berufsbegleitender Studienangebote: OHO-Arbeitsbericht*, https://w3-mediapool.hm.edu/mediapool/media/dachmarke/dm_lokal/oho/oho1/informationsmaterial/veroeffentlichungen_2/intern_3/ab_2_leitfaden_studiengangentwicklung.pdf. [1]

Notes

[1] In view of their specialised mandate, the two public higher education institutions in public administration were not invited to participate in the survey.

[2] It should be noted, however, that this is a so-called "should provision" (*Soll-Vorschrift*) in which – if supported by an appropriate justification – deviations are, in principle, possible. See also *BVerfG, Urteil vom* 28.02.1973 – VIII C 49/72, NJW 1973, 1206, 1207.

5 Recommendations

This chapter draws on the analysis in the earlier chapters to present a set of recommendations for how the Brandenburg state government and the state's HEIs might address the legal uncertainties they face. In particular, it presents a set of classification tools to be used by HEIs in the design and development of CET programmes to ensure that their classification of programmes meets EU state aid rules. It recommends to the state government the development of a guideline that will help HEIs minimise legal risk while the EU considers the request for a definitive ruling on the status of CET. It also provides proposals to the European Commission (EC) on how to clarify the application of European law to continuing education and training.

Introduction

Continuing education and training (CET) is identified in German law (as well as in the law of the federal state of Brandenburg) as a core task of higher education institutions (HEIs).

The digital transformation of the economy and the increasing digitalisation and automation of work mean that the skills and qualifications required for jobs have changed and are expected to change further (BMAS, 2020[1]). New skills are required by workers whose jobs will require them to work with new technologies. For example, the OECD predicts that more than 50% of all occupations in the German labour market will undergo fundamental change by 2030 (Nedelkoska and Quintini, 2018[2]). In particular, the increased use of artificial intelligence, robotics and virtual reality technology means that more and more occupations will require greater and changing skills.

In addition, the ageing of the population and improving health mean that people are expected to spend longer time in employment than in past, with the result that the population will need to make greater use of reskilling and upskilling opportunities. Therefore, providing better qualification and retraining opportunities for workers is an important priority for all governments, including the states of the German federal republic.

At the EU level, CET and other forms of lifelong learning are also seen as strategic political goals. The German Government has set itself the goal of promoting continuing education and training and lifelong learning more effectively (BMAS, 2020[1]). CET is also of critical importance to Brandenburg as it faces the challenges of demographic and economic change and the need to equip its workforce with more advanced and changing skills.

The OECD recommends lowering the barriers to further education and training, especially for underrepresented groups (OECD, 2021[3]). Reducing the barriers to CET may entail measures such as creating financial incentives, providing education and training leave for workers and recognising skills acquired in the workplace. In addition, the OECD considers it advisable to make CET more flexible, for example through the use of modular courses.

This makes it all the more important to establish arrangements for the funding of CET in higher education in ways that comply with EU state aid rules, since CET programmes are offered in a wide-ranging market by both public and private providers. As noted above, currently, how EU state aid rules apply to state-funded CET is unclear, despite a number of education-related decisions by the ECJ and the EC. Importantly, the ECJ has yet to hand down a judgment on the circumstances under which CET at HEIs can be classed as a non-economic activity in terms of the notion of an undertaking according to Art. 107(1) TFEU.

Nor do the KMK Guidelines create clarity in all cases and (as described in Chapter 3); they are seen as incomplete and narrowly framed. The Guidelines state:

> "The classification of continuing education and training at higher education institutions as an economic activity is viewed in a differentiated manner. In principle, where programmes are in competition with other programmes, especially those offered by private providers, it can be assumed that there is a market and that the activity is therefore economic. Particularly because German law consistently provides for the classification of continuing education as a statutory task of higher education institutions, but European law does not, auditors advise higher education institutions to always report continuing education and training as an economic activity". (KMK, 2017[4]).

The KMK's narrow approach is supported by the fact that the EC sees competition from private providers as, generally speaking, in favour of economic activity. However, it is not clear why the lack of uniform integration of CET into the state education system throughout Europe should be of decisive importance. The question also arises as to whether the Guidelines' assertion is justified by practice that, if the state funding of a CET programme is less than 50%, this leads it to be classified as an economic activity.

Ultimately, case law is decisive, as it is developed by the ECJ and the EC's administrative practice. Each CET offering must be examined individually on the basis of the criteria of case law and EC practice, as outlined in Chapter 3 of this report. Each offering needs to be assessed and then classified as economic or non-economic. It should be noted that these criteria are always subject to further development and improvement as a result of new decisions. Given that the publication of new decisions can take some time, it cannot be ruled out that isolated court or EC decisions may already have been handed down that contradict the statements made in this report.

To implement CET in conformity with EU state aid rules is the responsibility of the EC, the HEIs that offer CET, and, in Brandenburg, the Ministry for Science, Research and Culture (MWFK). Only the EU bodies have the power to create legal certainty when it comes to interpreting how the EU state aid rules apply to CET. However, a clarification regarding the classification of CET seems questionable, at least in the medium term. HEIs need therefore to take into account the evolving status of case law and the administrative practice of the EC in organising their CET offer so as to comply with state aid rules.

The recommendations in this report call on:

- the EC to clarify the application of the law to CET, thus creating legal certainty;
- Brandenburg's HEIs to follow the approach to classifying and organising their CET programmes based on the legal analysis in this report;
- MWFK to develop a guideline, consistent with the approach suggested in this report, that will help HEIs minimise legal risk while the EU considers the request for a definitive ruling on the status of CET.

Such a guideline would not necessarily be linked to the provision of new funding, but could be aimed at basic funding resources. It could outline the structure of a CET offering that complies with EU state aid rules and could also list the possible exceptions to the prohibition of state aid that may be applicable to CET offerings. It should then be notified to the EC within the framework of a (pre-)notification. The approval of a state aid practice by the EC appears to be a practically achievable way to create the greatest possible legal certainty for Brandenburg's HEIs.

The recommendations in this chapter are therefore addressed not only to the EC and Brandenburg's HEIs, but also to the MWFK. They lay out how the task of funding and implementing CET can be implemented in Brandenburg's higher education system, in compliance with state aid rules.

Proposal to the EC

One way to create legal certainty at the political level is to press the EC to clarify the classification of CET at HEIs[1]. This study proposes that EU state aid rules be simplified regarding CET programmes offered by public HEIs. The application of EU state aid rules is difficult to reconcile with the paramount importance of CET and the goal of boosting CET. It is therefore proposed that the possibility of funding CET be made simple and legally secure throughout the EU.

A viable approach could be to specifz in the Research & Development (R&D) Framework that CET at HEIs is a non-economic activity, in principle. It would also be desirable to clarify the criteria according to which CET at HEIs is to be classified as economic or non-economic. Finally, higher education institutions would benefit from a revision of the 20% clause – where an economic activity is deemed fundable if it consumes the same inputs as the principal (non-economic) activity and represents no more than 20% of the total activity – leading to a more straightforward applicability. The current R&D Framework states only that the extent of economic operations will be monitored for a period of 10 years (EC, 2021[5]).

Standardisation of the individual case assessment at HEIs

Given:

- the legal uncertainties in the assessment of the application of the EU state aid rules to CET;
- the fact that the R&D Framework is still in draft;
- the ongoing disputes about the exact criteria for the classification of CET offerings;
- the likelihood that resolution of these problems will be protracted;

there is a need for an interim solution to the legal issues posed by CET. This report recommends the following steps for the assessment of an individual CET offering in the interest of risk management.

These recommendations are given on the basis of case law and the assessment practice of the EC, as described in Chapter 3 of this report. The constant development of EU state aid rules means that these standards may change, however; case law and assessment practice may differ over time from that cited here, requiring a different evaluation. The result is that every individual CET offering is to be treated as a separate case in terms of state rules standards; the following can only be seen as orientation assistance valid at the time of writing.

Step 1: Assessment of EU state aid rules in terms of constitutive conditions

The following assessment chart (Figure 5.1) is intended to provide guidance on the criteria to be reviewed when classifying a CET offering. It does this by looking, in order, at the elements that constitute compliance with state aid conditions.

Figure 5.1. Assessment chart for HEIs on the criteria to be reviewed when classifying a CET offering

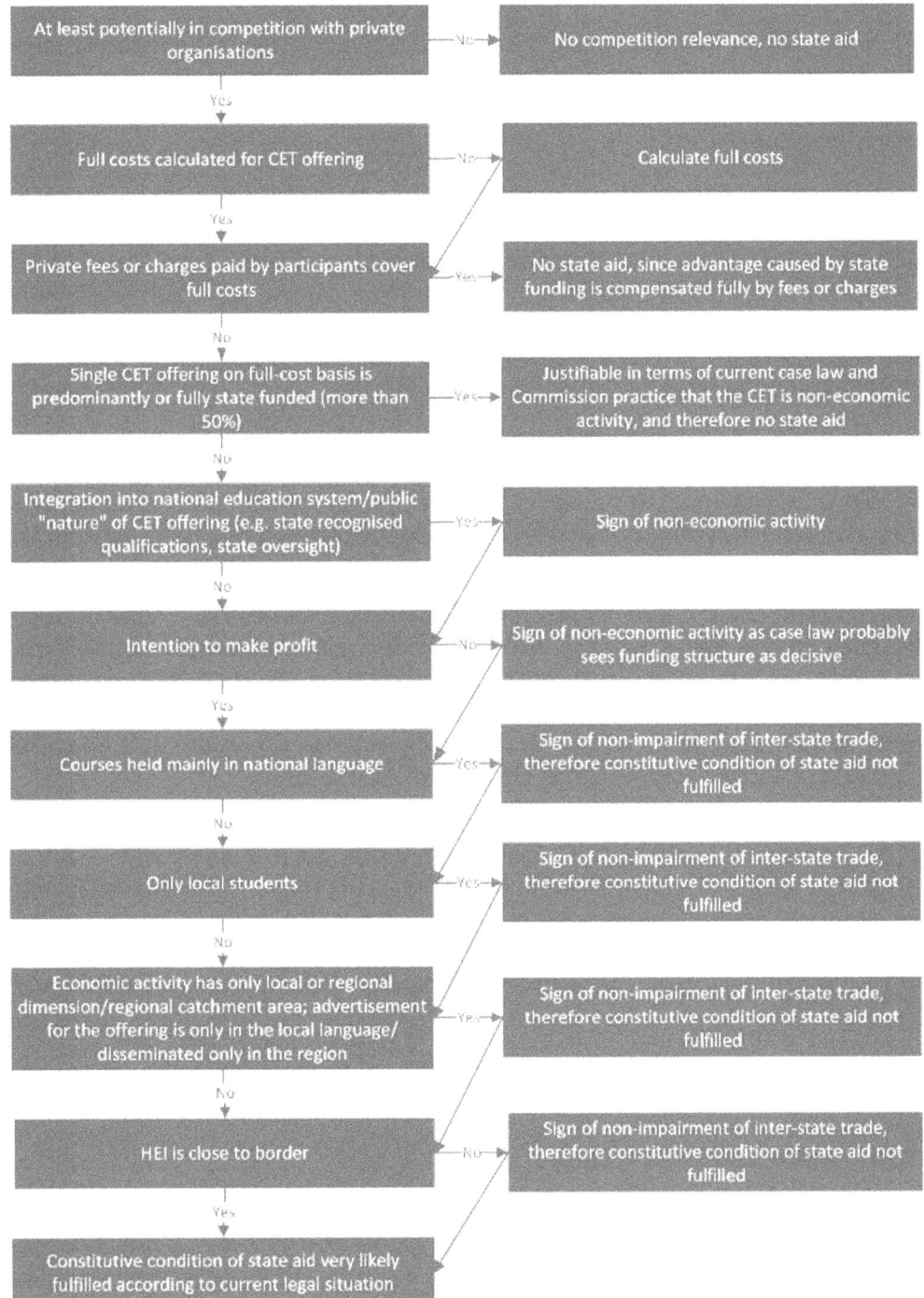

Step 2: If constitutive conditions of state aid are fulfilled, assess the possibility of exception and justification

If the assessment of a CET offering shows that the course does meet the conditions for the receipt of state aid, the prohibition of state aid in Art. 107(1) TFEU does not apply. If this is not the case, exceptions and exemption possibilities may be investigated.

De minimis and SGEI de minimis aid

One exception to the prohibition of state aid frequently applied in practice is *de minimis* aid and Services of General Economic Interest (SGEI) *de minimis* aid. *De minimis* aid is aid that does not exceed a total amount of EUR 200 000 (or EUR 500 000 in the case of SGEI) paid to one undertaking (and its related undertakings) over a three-year period (EC, 2013[6]). Given these low thresholds, *de minimis* aid is often not likely to cover the entire costs of CET offered by a HEI. Nevertheless, this type of aid can provide funding flexibility for HEIs.

General Block Exemption Regulation

Individual CET offerings could also fall within one of the exemptions listed in the General Block Exemption Regulation (GBER) (Nowak, 2016[7]) and could be permitted to receive state aid. The offering could be assessed to see if it meets the conditions of training aid (Art. 31 GBER), aid to compensate for the costs of supporting disadvantaged workers (Art. 35 GBER), aid for culture and heritage conservation (Art. 53 GBER) or start-up aid (Art. 22 GBER).

Training aid is aid granted to undertakings to train their own workforce, with the exception of training that is compulsory for the undertaking (such as safety training). If an undertaking uses CET offered by a HEI, 50% of the costs (70% under certain conditions) can be covered by aid, leading to a lower price being charged by the HEI. Note, however, that, in this case, the general requirements of Chapters I and II of the GBER (in particular transparency, Art. 5 GBER and incentive effect, Art. 6 GBER) must be observed.

There is also provision under GBER for aid for training personnel needed to support disadvantaged workers (Art. 35 GBER), as well as for CET courses that deal with cultural heritage, customs and crafts (Art. 53(2)(c) GBER), or with cultural and artistic education, (Art. 53(2)(e) GBER) such as continuing musical education. In the case of cultural aid within the meaning of Art. 53(2)(e) GBER, orientation can be found n the relevant EC decision on a Spanish music school, whose services could be partially publicly funded without being classified as state aid on the basis of Art. 53 GBER.

Start-up aid under Art. 22 GBER could be used in cases where the CET is to be provided by a newly established undertaking. That part of GBER does not, however, apply if the newly founded undertaking was established as a result of a merger. Further, the Brandenburg Higher Education Act (BbgHG) permits only the organisational implementation and marketing of the CET offering to be carried out by a co-operative undertaking; the HEI must always retain a controlling influence over the undertaking. Thus, the HEI and the start-up undertaking are related undertakings (Art. 3(3) Annex I GBER) and funding is precluded.

If a CET offering fulfils the above-mentioned conditions, whether it meets the general and specific requirements of the GBER should be checked.

R&D Framework and the 20% clause

The 20% clause – where an economic activity is deemed fundable if it consumes the same inputs as the principal (non-economic) activity and represents no more than 20% of the total activity – could offer an argument for an exception. The EC is currently revising the clause to make it more manageable and to eliminate legal uncertainties. Based on the 20% clause, all economic activities of the higher education institution can be classified as non-economic activities, provided that the economic activities are only of minor importance, that no additional inputs are required and that the 20% threshold is not exceeded (cf. Point 20 of the R&D Framework).

CET as a Service of General Economic Interest

An exception to the prohibition of state aid may be possible in individual cases if the aid for CET is structured as a Service of General Economic Interest (SGEI). The definition of an SGEI was concretised (among other things) by the EC's decision on the exemption of SGEI aid (2012/21/EU) of 20 December 2011 (SGEI Exemption Decision) (EC, 2012[8]). The decision is applicable if the annual average compensation does not exceed EUR 15 million (cf. Art. 2(1)(a) SGEI Exemption Decision).

This concerns state aid that is granted to compensate for the loss-making provision of "services of general economic interest" (EC, 2012[9]) (EC, 2013[10]) by an undertaking which has been entrusted by the state to provide those services. The existence of an SGEI must be justified on the basis of concrete circumstances. These include that the service may not be in the commercial interest of the undertaking providing the service, but must be in the interest of the general public and therefore would not be provided by the undertaking if it were not entrusted with the provision of the service, or at least not to the same extent or under the same conditions. This can be assumed on a case-by-case basis for CET services – with a comprehensive justification related to the individual case.

The definition of a service as being of "general economic interest" by the Member State is only subject to limited review by the EC. However, the act of entrustment carries legal uncertainty. The act of entrustment is a sovereign act by the Member State; it has the effect of transferring responsibility for provision of a service of general economic interest to an undertaking. The act of entrustment, which usually takes the form of an administrative act or a contract under public law, must according to Art. 4 of the SGEI Exemption Decision in any case contain information on the following elements:

- the subject and duration of the public service obligations;
- the undertaking and, if applicable, the area concerned;
- the nature of any exclusive or special rights granted to the undertaking by the consenting authority;
- description of the compensation mechanism and parameters for the calculation, monitoring and revision of the compensatory payments;
- measures to avoid and recover excess compensation payments.

The calculation of the net additional costs (and thus the permissible amount of aid) requires a detailed description. The act of entrustment must specify the calculations (turnover and income from the SGEI, minus the total costs incurred and a reasonable profit on the capital employed, and the compensatory payments) and statements on how excess compensation will be avoided must be presented.

In addition, the undertaking receiving the SGEI aid must be obliged to keep separate accounts for the SGEI service (in accordance with Art. 5(9) SGEI Exemption Decision). There are also requirements under the SGEI Exemption Decision which must be assessed on a case-by-case basis.

These extensive regulations pose considerable challenges in practice. Nevertheless, the SGEI approach could be considered in those areas that are strongly affected by the ongoing structural changes or in those areas where training a qualified workforce is particularly in the public interest. For example, CET programmes in the social and medical care sectors could be considered. The public interest here could be to train sufficiently qualified personnel at affordable costs in Brandenburg and to bind them to the state as workers in the medium and long term.

Step 3: Set prices in conformity with EU state aid rules

Avoid indirect aid when co-operating with commercial undertakings by setting prices in conformity with EU state aid rules

When a HEI co-operates with a commercial undertaking to offer CET, the prices charged need to be set in conformity with EU state aid rules in order to avoid aid favouring the commercial partner or other enterprises. If the co-operation between the HEI and a commercial undertaking is classified as an economic activity, then the HEI needs to set a price that covers the full costs plus a margin for profit or else it must set the price at a market price (that covers at least the full costs). In this way, the HEI can avoid aid being granted to the commercial undertaking and itself.

The use of overhead costs in calculating full costs

Overhead costs include the costs of administration and usage of central facilities and premises. Depreciation of fixed assets that cannot be clearly allocated to a specific project is considered as well.

The overhead costs are allocated to the individual projects using an overhead surcharge rate. A HEI has some discretion in determining this surcharge rate with regard to the reference value to be selected and the level at which the overhead rates are formed. A survey of HEIs showed that the majority of Brandenburg's HEIs apply the same overhead cost rate for research services and CET. This should be reviewed by each HEI because CET may impose lower costs on institutional facilities and administration than research projects. For example, infrastructure costs account for only a small proportion of CET costs. Horst Rambau, a tax expert (*Steuerberater*) who has expertise in HEI operations, advised the OECD that an overhead cost rate of 25% may be realistic for CET.

Step 4: Documentation

All essential decision-making steps and justifications must be comprehensively documented within the HEI in case of possible administrative proceedings under state aid rules. This applies, above all, to the classification of CET programmes as non-economic or economic activities, but also to the price calculation and the use of exceptions and possible justifications.

Developing a guideline for the *Land* Brandenburg

The discussion above shows that, in principle, it is possible for CET programmes offered by HEIs to be funded by the state without the funding being classified as prohibited state aid. The difficulties arise from the fact that the application of EU state aid rules to publicly-funded CET programmes lacks clarity, raising legal uncertainty. Expecting complete clarification from the EU bodies appears unrealistic, in the medium term at least, meaning that the HEIs are unable to categorise their CET programmes with legal certainty. In this situation, it is possible for the state of Brandenburg to establish a guideline to clarify when HEIs may use state funding to subsidise CET.

Given the many different forms of CET at HEIs, the content of a guideline can only be sketched here. The guideline should indicate that the use of state funding for non-economic CET is permitted. Secondly, the guideline should set out the circumstances under which state funding can be used for CET that has been classified as an economic activity (see Criteria 1 and 2 below).

In addition, the guideline should specify the cases for which an official administrative decision would need to be issued and those in which a notice by the HEI would be sufficient.

Criterion 1: Non-economic nature of the CET

The guideline could first clarify that CET programmes can be offered using state-funded infrastructure and/or state-funded personnel if the CET programme does not fulfil the criteria for the prohibition on state aid. On the basis of the case law and EC practice described in this report, the Brandenburg state government could make fulfilment of the following three criteria essential:

- The CET programme is integrated into the public higher education system (see below).
- Fees paid cover a maximum of 49.9% of the full costs of the CET programme.
- There is no competition.

A more differentiated approach is also possible, in principle. However, the more differentiated the structure, the more difficult notification might be.

Integration in the public higher education system

The question of how a CET programme is integrated into the state education system is a criterion used by the EC. The KMK Guidelines also use this criterion.

A CET programme to be funded is integrated into the public higher education system if it contributes to fulfilling the state mandate to provide CET by state institutions that are subject to state recognition and state oversight. If applicable, it should also be noted that state degrees are awarded (e.g. master's degrees) and that the higher education institutions in Brandenburg remain responsible for content and examinations even when co-operating with non-university institutions (§ 25(4) BbgHG).

The following wording is suggested:

> "The continuing education and training programme to be funded serves the fulfilment of a state mandate for the provision of continuing education and training by state institutions that are subject to state recognition and state oversight."

Funding

As can be seen from the case studies in the KMK Guidelines, another important criterion is the funding structure of the CET programme in question. Case law suggests that funding that is (at least) substantially provided through public resources indicates that the programme can be argued to be a non-economic activity[2] (although in the absence of sufficiently clear case law, it cannot be ruled out that the economic character can also be present despite substantial state funding).

In order to exclude the possibility of state aid with any legal certainty, a "substantial" level of state funding can be defined for the CET programme. Neither the ECJ nor the EC specify what can be considered as "substantial" state funding. The literature on CET suggests that state funding of more than 50% of the full costs for a particular programme is to be considered "substantial" in the terms of the ECJ case law (Marwedel, 2014[11])[3]. This is also in line with the KMK Guidelines.

The following wording is suggested:

> "At least 50.1 % of the eligible full costs of the continuing education and training programme to be funded will be provided through public subsidy."

Criterion 2: Exceptions to the prohibition of state aid

In a second step, the guideline could specify the conditions under which state funding can also be used for a CET programme not covered by the prohibition of state aid under Criterion 1. Here, too, all of the exceptions listed in this report can be used. In the interest of simplicity, this report recommends focusing on selected exceptions: training aid, services of general economic interest (SGEI) aid, *de minimis* aid and the use of the 20% clause appear plausible.

Training aid

Aid exempted under the GBER can be mentioned in the guideline as being in conformity with EU state aid rules. According to Art. 31 GBER, for example, a grant may be awarded as exempted training aid. This can be included in the proposed guideline:

> *"Under the conditions of Article 31 GBER, the grant may be awarded as exempted training aid. Measures which, according to Article 31(2) GBER, serve to help undertakings comply with mandatory training standards are excluded from exemption under this exception."*

SGEI

Continuing education and training programmes that are deemed economically viable under Criterion 1 may be partially funded by the state in isolated cases if they are classified as SGEI. However, only the additional costs incurred by the higher education institution due to the provision of the CET programme are eligible for funding. Provision of an SGEI could be justified, for example, by the fact that the CET is intended to increase the training capacity in the state of Brandenburg.

The following wording could be used in the proposed guideline:

> *"Continuing education and training measures which cannot be funded in accordance with the aforementioned regulations may be partially funded by the state on a case-by-case basis if the higher education institution is entrusted with the provision of the continuing education and training measure as a "service of general economic interest" (SGEI).*
>
> *SGEI requires that the applicant is entrusted in writing with the provision of services of general economic interest and that the provision of the CET offering in question is a service of general economic interest. The compensation of losses incurred by the HEIs through the provision of the respective CET programme is then considered free of aid. However, only the additional costs incurred by the HEI due to the provision of the CET programme are eligible for funding."*

De Minimis *Regulation*

The proposed guideline should also make reference to the possibility of funding under the *De Minimis* Regulation.

The following wording is proposed:

> *"Funding without the above-mentioned conditions is possible on the basis of the* De Minimis *Regulation. This requires that the sum of the grants does not exceed a cumulative amount of EUR 200 000 over a period of three fiscal years."*

Other CET offerings: The 20% rule

Grants for CET measures are, in principle, also permissible under EU state aid rules if existing infrastructure and human resources are only used to 20% of their availability. It is therefore necessary to include a clarifying wording in the proposed guideline. The below proposal is based on the wording of the 20% clause in the R&D guidelines:

> *"Funding without the above restrictions is possible in accordance with Point 20 R&D Framework if the same inputs (such as materials, equipment, personnel and fixed capital) are used for the CET programme classified as an economic activity as are used for the HEIs' non-economic activities and if the annual capacity allocated to the economic activity in question does not exceed 20% of the total annual capacity of the institution or infrastructure concerned."*

It would be advisable to include a set of worked examples of this abstract regulation in the proposed guideline. It would also be advisable to make a corresponding understanding of the clause the subject of the notification.

Pre-notification, notification and registration of the guideline to the EC

In order to achieve the greatest possible legal certainty for a new guideline set up by the state of Brandenburg, the guideline should be pre-notified, notified or registered to the EC.

Art. 108(3) TFEU stipulates that notification to the EC is required only for measures that meet all the criteria of Art. 107(1) TFEU and thus constitute prohibited state aid (Callies/Ruffert, 2016[12]). However, if the EC declares the aid compatible with the common market in the notification procedure, the aid is permitted.

In view of the serious legal consequences of aid being implemented without the necessary notification, it may make sense in individual cases to notify an intended measure as "not state aid". The notification is made using the same standard form as for notification as aid. The standard form explicitly provides the option for notification as not state aid (EC, 2004[13]). A notification as not state aid will relate to measures where the state aid character is difficult to determine, such as when there are complex economic considerations with regard to pricing in conformity with EU state aid rules. In practice, the EC often suggests withdrawal of the notification as not state aid if, after a preliminary examination, it does not consider the measure to meet the threshold for the prohibition of state aid. This gives the HEIs only limited legal certainty, but it should at least protect them from a claim for recovery (Bacon, 2017[14]) (EC, 2011[15])[4].

The notification procedure of the guideline to the EC is outlined in Box 5.1.

Box 5.1. Procedure of the notification of the guideline to the EC

The **notification** procedure is governed by Article 108 (3) TFEU in conjunction with the Procedural Regulation issued for this purpose (Regulation 2015/1589 of 13 July 2015, OJ EU L 248) (Council of the European Union, 2015[16]).

Pre-notification involves presenting the proposal in question, and the assessment of it under state aid rules, to the EC in advance of notification. This usually involves a meeting of all parties involved at the EC's headquarters in Brussels.

Pre-notification is an informal procedural step that is not explicitly provided for in the Procedural Regulation, but it corresponds to the usual procedure. This phase provides the opportunity for discussion of questions about the scope and design of the notification application and questions from the EC about the proposal to be discussed. The basis for the discussion should be a draft of the notification application that has already been substantially drafted, and which can ideally be adjusted without major effort, on the basis of the information gained from the discussion. Therefore, the necessary economic and legal analyses and the notification application (consisting of a proposal and an assessment) should be prepared in draft form in advance of the meeting.

The final notification application, revised on the basis of the information gained from the pre-notification meeting and agreed between the parties, is then submitted to the EC by the German Government through its representation in Brussels. This step marks the beginning of the official notification process.

In the notification process itself, the EC initiates a **preliminary examination procedure** (Art. 4 Procedural Regulation) by examining, on the basis of the notification, whether state aid has been granted and, if so, whether the intended aid is compatible with the single market.

The preliminary examination procedure usually involves one or two requests for further information by the EC (Art. 5 Regulation). For this purpose, questions are sent by the EC to the Permanent Representation of the Federal Republic of Germany to the European Union, which forwards them to the actual parties involved via the responsible department at the federal level.

If the EC affirms compatibility, it can issue an approval decision after the preliminary examination procedure.

If there are serious doubts as to the compatibility of the aid with the common market and if these doubts are not dispelled by the rounds of questions, the EC may initiate a **formal investigation procedure** (Art. 6 Procedural Regulation), which serves the purpose of an in-depth examination, including the views of third parties.

As part of the in-depth examination, the EC publishes the initial decision of the aid recipient and the preliminary assessment by the EC in the Official Journal of the EU and invites other EU Member States and competitors of the aid recipient to comment. The EC may also address further questions to the Member State and request it to submit additional information. At the end of the formal investigation procedure, there is either **an approval resolution** (possibly subject to conditions) **or a resolution** declaring the planned aid incompatible with the common market.

A first response from the EC can, in principle, be expected after two months (cf. Art. 4(5) Procedural Regulation). According to Art. 9(6) Regulation, the maximum duration of the notification procedure should not exceed 18 months. A duration of six months seems realistic.

Sources: Callies/Ruffert (ed.) (2016[12]), *TEU/TFEU, 5. Auflage 2016*; Council of the European Union (2015[16]), Council Regulation (EU) 2015/1589 of 13 July 2015 laying down detailed rules for the application of Article 108 of the Treaty on the Functioning of the European Union (Text with EEA relevance), OJ L 248, 24.9.2015.

References

Bacon (2017), *European Union Law of State Aid*, Oxford University Press. [14]

BMAS (2020), *Nationale Weiterbildungsstrategie*, https://www.bmas.de/DE/Arbeit/Aus-und-Weiterbildung/Weiterbildung/Nationale-Weiterbildungsstrategie/nationale-weiterbildungsstrategie.html. [1]

Callies/Ruffert (ed.) (2016), *TEU/TFEU, 5. Auflage 2016*. [12]

Council of the European Union (2015), *Council Regulation (EU) 2015/1589 of 13 July 2015 laying down detailed rules for the application of Article 108 of the Treaty on the Functioning of the European Union (Text with EEA relevance), OJ L 248, 24.9.2015.*. [16]

EC (2021), *Review of the Communication on the Framework for State aid for research and development and innovation*, https://ec.europa.eu/competition-policy/public-consultations/2021-rdi_en. [5]

EC (2013), *Commission Regulation (EU) No 1407/2013 of 18.12.2013 on the application of Articles 107 and 108 of the Treaty on the Functioning of the European Union to de minimis aid.* [6]

EC (2013), *Guide to the application of the European Union rules on state aid, public procurement and the internal market to services of general economic interest, and in particular to social services of general interest, of 29.04.2013, SWD(2013) 53 final/2.* [10]

EC (2012), *Commission Decision of 20 December 2011, 2012/21/EU.* [8]

EC (2012), *Communication from the Commission — European Union framework for State aid in the form of public service compensation (2011) Text with EEA relevance.* [9]

EC (2011), *Commission decision 2011/5/EC, OJ 2011 L7/48.* [15]

EC (2004), *Commission Regulation (EC) No. 794/2004 of 21 April 2004 implementing Council Regulation (EC) No. 659/1999 laying down detailed rules for the application of Article 93 of the EC Treaty.* [13]

Immenga/Mestmäcker (ed.) (2016), *Wettbewerbsrecht, 5. Auflage*. [7]

KMK (2017), *Leitfaden zur Unterscheidung wirtschaftlicher und nichtwirtschaftlicher Tätigkeit von Hochschulen*, https://www.kmk.org/fileadmin/Dateien/veroeffentlichungen_beschluesse/2017/2017_09_22-Leitfaden-Wirt-. [4]

Marwedel (2014), *Rechtsgutachten zu Vorgaben für die Preisgestaltung der wissenschaftlichen Weiterbildung an der Universität Freiburg unter besonderer Berücksichtigung des europäischen Beihilferechts*, [Legal opinion on specifications for the pricing of scientific further education at the University of Freiburg with special consideration of European state aid law]. [11]

Nedelkoska, L. and G. Quintini (2018), "Automation, skills use and training", *OECD Social, Employment and Migration Working Papers*, No. 202, OECD Publishing, Paris, https://dx.doi.org/10.1787/2e2f4eea-en. [2]

OECD (2021), *Continuing Education and Training in Germany*, Getting Skills Right, OECD Publishing, Paris, https://dx.doi.org/10.1787/1f552468-en. [3]

Notes

[1] It should be noted, however, that the European Commission has only limited scope in this area. The European courts are the bodies, which can provide definite clarification on the classification of CET.

[2] ECJ judgement in the Wirth case – see Box 3.1 in Chapter 3.

[3] Marwedel, Rechtsgutachten zu Vorgaben für die Preisgestaltung der wissenschaftlichen Weiterbildung an der Universität Freiburg unter besonderer Berücksichtigung des europäischen Beihilferechts, 2014, p. 27.

[4] See Commission Regulation (EC) No. 794/2004 of 21 April 2004 implementing Council Regulation (EC) No. 659/1999 laying down detailed rules for the application of Article 93 of the EC Treaty.

Annex A. Cost accounting approaches

Background

Chapter 3 of this report discussed the fact that, if an HEI undertakes an economic activity, it must levy market-appropriate charges for the use of its infrastructure and staffing in the delivery of that activity.

A market-appropriate charge is one that is sufficient to meet all of the costs of the activity, to ensure that there is no subsidy from state funding. That means the charge must cover the operational costs, the costs of capital, a return on equity and an appropriate mark-up or margin for profit.

Chapter 3 discussed the fact that charges may be differentiated between different services (such as different CET programmes), or the HEI may choose to offer all CET programmes at a flat rate.

This annex sets out the approaches that a HEI might use to ensure it complies with the requirement to avoid cross subsidy and to ensure that the economic activity does not receive a "favour" in the market and hence, does not distort the operation of the market and does not impair trade.

Permissibility of the "backwards from the end" approach

In practice, flat-rate charges are determined "backwards from the end". This approach appears to be justifiable on good grounds. In simple terms, calculating "backwards from the end" means that an undertaking determines the project costs and charges them to the client with a mark-up of, for example, 8%. The flat-rate charge is then passed on to the HEI. This means that the HEI has no possibility of exercising "forward control", i.e. checking the accuracy of the determination and increasing the flat-rate charge, if necessary, in advance. The HEI discovers the flat-rate charge only after the project has been completed and invoiced.

This problem recalls the determination of transfer prices between a parent undertaking and a subsidiary where the parent undertaking provides services to the subsidiary and the subsidiary provides a finished product or a service on that basis. This raises the question of the correct transfer price, particularly from the point of view of taxation.

As part of the 2008 corporate tax reform, Germany stipulated that if there are fully comparable "arm's length" values, the appropriate transfer price must be determined primarily according to the business case-related standard methods (§ 1(3) AStG [Taxation of Foreign Relations Act, *Gesetzes über die Besteuerung von Auslandsbeziehungen*]).

These standard methods are:

- the price comparison method;
- the resale price method;
- the cost-plus method.

These methods, shaped by tax law, fundamentally have no relevance for EU state aid rules. However, if they have become commonly used in business in Germany, even for tax reasons, then this practice will play a role in the economic aspects of EU state aid rules.

- The **price comparison method** – also known as the Comparable Uncontrolled Price Method (CUP) – is considered to be the standard method for determining transfer prices due to the immediacy with which the comparison price can be established. The method is to compare the price agreed for transactions between related parties with the price agreed for similar transactions between independent third parties (or between related parties and an independent third party who cannot be influenced by decisions made by the company or company owners (Vögele/Raab, 2015[1]))[1]. In other words, the appropriate transfer price is determined on the basis of comparable transactions between a service provider and an independent service recipient. The prerequisite for using the price comparison method is that the prices for the transaction in question are fully, or at least partially, comparable with those of the transaction drawn on for comparison.
- The **cost-plus method** (CPM) determines the appropriate transfer price in a two-step process. Based on the assumption that the manufacturing cost of a product or a performance represents its intrinsic exchange value, the cost price of the providing party is used as the starting point and an appropriate mark-up (a proxy for profit) is added (Vögele/Raab, 2015[1])[2]. The underlying idea behind the CPM is that a commercial enterprise can be economically viable in the long term only if its full costs (both variable and fixed costs) are covered and if a certain minimum profit can be achieved. This principle is also the foundation of the above norms of EU state aid.
- The **resale price method** (RPM) takes as its starting point the price for which an undertaking sells goods it has acquired from a related undertaking in the group to an independent purchaser. The starting point of the RPM is thus the price that the resale undertaking obtains on the market. The price of sale is reduced by a fair-market margin, the size of which is determined by the following three components: i) the costs incurred by the reseller; ii) the functions and risks assumed by the reseller during the supply or performance relationship with the related party; and iii) a reasonable profit mark-up for the reseller.

This last method – which is also recognised in Germany – can thus be said to think "backwards from the end", meaning that the approach is not completely devoid of economic foundations. As EU state rules also use a "backwards from the end" approach, the basic approach of the RPM method does not seem unreasonable.

Assessment in accordance with the principles of separate accounting

Even if it is permissible to use the approach of flat-rate charges, this does not mean that the flat-rate charge applied in an actual case or the basis of its calculation are reasonable. Each individual case needs to be assessed.

In this respect, all parties involved at the HEI will have to observe the principle of proper separate accounting. Essential elements of separate accounting are correct full-cost accounting and correct cost allocation. If a market price is not known for the economic activities of the HEI, it is important that the calculation of the quotation includes total costs with a profit mark-up. Full-cost accounting is a suitable cost-accounting system for ensuring that total cost is recognised. It consists of the following three components:

- **Cost type accounting**: Which costs have been incurred?
- **Cost centre accounting**: Where did the costs arise? The structure of cost centre accounting is based on the organisational units of the HEI (departments, institutions, etc.).
- **Cost unit accounting**: What were the costs incurred for? The individual projects and contracts are to be recorded as cost units.

It is well known in practice at HEIs, and especially in auditors' reports, that the costing must take place in several steps.

Preliminary costing

Anyone who engages in economic activities must, as a matter of principle, cost them in advance. This is a requirement in the sense of Point 25 of the R&D Framework, which assumes in the case of research services by an HEI – and *mutatis mutandi* also in the case of other economic activities by the HEI – *ex ante* costing (and not *ex post*, i.e. only after the project has been carried out).

The preliminary costing within the framework of the separate accounting includes direct and indirect costs, i.e. according to general principles, the costs directly attributable to an expected project are recorded and calculated with the internal overhead surcharge determined in-house by the HEI. This then results in a total price, which – with a profit mark-up – forms the basis of the calculation.

Final costing

In final costing, the **actual costs incurred** and **actual revenues** are compared with each other. When determining the actual costs, it should be noted that the overhead costs taken into account are not allocated using the overhead rates used in preliminary costing, but on the basis of the actual costs.

The HEI must be able to make a final cost calculation. To do this, the HEI may also need the co-operating undertaking to supply a statement of costs from which it is possible for the HEI to check whether the cost estimates were retrospectively correct in the relevant year, thus making it possible to adjust them for the future. This is crucial also because final costing has an impact on preliminary costing. This is because, if it becomes clear that the *ex ante* costing is no longer appropriate because the use of resources developed significantly differently than costed and was more intensive, then, from the point of view of EU state rules described above, the HEI must adjust its future costing.

References

Vögele/Borstell/Engeler (ed.) (2015), *Verrechnungspreise, 4. Auflage.* [1]

Notes

[1] *Vögele/Raab* in: Vögele/Borstell/Engeler, *Verrechnungspreise, 4. Auflage* 2015, *Kapitel D.* marginal 50 ff.

[2] *Vögele/Raab* in: Vögele/Borstell/Engeler, *Verrechnungspreise, 4. Auflage* 2015, *Kapitel D.* marginal 250 ff.

www.ingramcontent.com/pod-product-compliance
Ingram Content Group UK Ltd.
Pitfield, Milton Keynes, MK11 3LW, UK
UKHW050412240426
12048UKWH00020B/1478